CHILD ABUSE
TRAGEDY AND TRAUMA

By Allison Krumsiek

Portions of this book originally appeared in *Child Abuse* by Bonnie Juettner.

LUCENT
PRESS

Published in 2018 by
Lucent Press, an Imprint of Greenhaven Publishing, LLC
353 3rd Avenue
Suite 255
New York, NY 10010

Designer: Andrea Davison-Bartolotta
Editor: Jessica Moore

Library of Congress Cataloging-in-Publication Data

Names: Krumsiek, Allison, author.
Title: Child abuse : tragedy and trauma / Allison Krumsiek.
Description: New York : Lucent Press, [2018] | Series: Hot topics | Includes
  bibliographical references and index.
Identifiers: LCCN 2017043556| ISBN 9781534562035 (library bound book) | ISBN
  9781534562905 (paperback book) | ISBN 9781534562042 (eBook)
Subjects: LCSH: Child abuse–United States. | Child abuse–Psychological
  aspects–United States.
Classification: LCC RC569.5.C55 K78 2018 | DDC 362.760973–dc23
LC record available at https://lccn.loc.gov/2017043556

CPSIA compliance information: Batch #CW18KL: For further information contact Greenhaven Publishing LLC, New York,
New York at 1-844-317-7404.

Please visit our website, www.greenhavenpublishing.com. For a free color catalog of all our
high-quality books, call toll free 1-844-317-7404 or fax 1-844-317-7405.

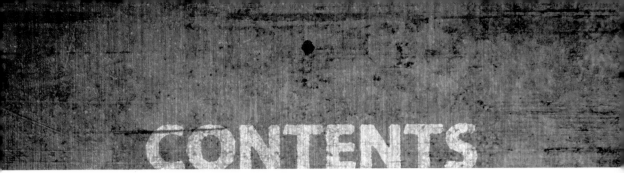

CONTENTS

FOREWORD   4

INTRODUCTION   6
Home Can Be a Dangerous Place

CHAPTER 1   11
Child Abuse in the United States

CHAPTER 2   26
Abuse at Any Age

CHAPTER 3   40
Investigating Child Abuse

CHAPTER 4   58
Preventing Child Abuse

CHAPTER 5   72
Healing Old Wounds

NOTES   90

DISCUSSION QUESTIONS   93

ORGANIZATIONS TO CONTACT   95

FOR MORE INFORMATION   97

INDEX   99

PICTURE CREDITS   103

ABOUT THE AUTHOR   104

Adolescence is a time when many people begin to take notice of the world around them. News channels, blogs, and talk radio shows are constantly promoting one view or another; very few are unbiased. Young people also hear conflicting information from parents, friends, teachers, and acquaintances. Often, they will hear only one side of an issue or be given flawed information. People who are trying to support a particular viewpoint may cite inaccurate facts and statistics on their blogs, and news programs present many conflicting views of important issues in our society. In a world where it seems everyone has a platform to share their thoughts, it can be difficult to find unbiased, accurate information about important issues.

It is not only facts that are important. In blog posts, in comments on online videos, and on talk shows, people will share opinions that are not necessarily true or false, but can still have a strong impact. For example, many young people struggle with their body image. Seeing or hearing negative comments about particular body types online can have a huge effect on the way someone views himself or herself and may lead to depression and anxiety. Although it is important not to keep information hidden from young people under the guise of protecting them, it is equally important to offer encouragement on issues that affect their mental health.

The titles in the Hot Topics series provide readers with different viewpoints on important issues in today's society. Many of these issues, such as teen pregnancy and Internet safety, are of immediate concern to young people. This series aims to give readers factual context on these crucial topics in a way that lets them form their own opinions. The facts presented throughout also serve to empower readers to help themselves or support people they know who are struggling with many of the challenges adolescents face today. Although negative viewpoints are not ignored or downplayed, this series allows young people to see that the challenges they face are not insurmountable. Eating disorders can be overcome, the Internet can be navigated safely, and pregnant teens do not have to feel hopeless.

Quotes encompassing all viewpoints are presented and cited so readers can trace them back to their original source, verifying for themselves whether the information comes from a reputable place. Additional books and websites are listed, giving readers a starting point from which to continue their own research. Chapter questions encourage discussion, allowing young people to hear and understand their classmates' points of view as they further solidify their own. Full-color photographs and enlightening charts provide a deeper understanding of the topics at hand. All of these features augment the informative text, helping young people understand the world they live in and formulate their own opinions concerning the best way they can improve it.

Home Can Be a Dangerous Place

For many children, home is a safe, healthy place to live. Home means security—a place where their needs are met and they feel loved. It is a place where family members are happy for them when they have a good day and support them when they experience challenges. Home is a refuge, a place to be themselves.

However, for thousands of children every year, home is anything but a refuge. Some children—more than 75,000 in 2014—live in homes where their needs are not met. Their homes do not always have food in the refrigerator. They may not have adequate clothes to wear. Their parents do not take them to the doctor when they need medical care. These children are neglected.

Other children—more than 17,000 in 2014—cannot trust their families or caretakers to be kind to them. Sometimes, their family members physically hurt them. Adults may strike or burn them, slam their fingers in doors, expose them to dangerous chemicals, or sexually abuse them. Some adults try to hurt children by forcing them to stay outside for hours in severely cold weather without warm clothes or shoes. They may try to scare a child by driving recklessly, or they may interrupt the child's sleep, causing the child to be tired during the day. Some adults have even attacked children with weapons.

Younger children are more likely to be abused than older kids. Some adults become so frustrated with a baby's cries that they shake the baby, causing physical harm, such as brain

Home is not always a safe place for a child.

damage or death. At other times, adults have violent reactions to the normal behavior of toddlers and preschoolers. Sometimes, children are tied up or locked in cages or confined spaces.

Physical abuse and neglect can occur simultaneously. In August 2008, state troopers in Michigan pulled over a car and found a four-week-old baby and his teenage parents inside. The baby had a pacifier taped to his mouth, which was physical abuse. The baby was also not in a car seat, which is considered neglect. The troopers arranged for the baby to be temporarily placed in the custody of his grandparents. Meanwhile, the Michigan Department of Human Services provided parenting classes to help the teenagers learn how to care for a baby.

Many children—more than 6,000 in 2014—are abused not just physically, but also psychologically. Their parents belittle them with verbal put-downs or threaten them. They may constantly call a child dumb or make fun of a child's appearance, or they may find ways to humiliate the child. For example, a 15-year-old living in Anchorage, Alaska, told an interviewer that when she was in fourth grade, her mother would arrive at her school drunk, pull her out of her classroom, and scream at her and at her teachers in front of other students. This type of abuse—emotional abuse—is sometimes referred to as "invisible child abuse" because it does not leave scars on the body. However, that does not mean it is not harmful.

Physical abuse and emotional abuse are not always separate. Physical abuse does cause emotional, as well as physical, injuries. However, social workers also investigate some cases in which children are abused emotionally but not physically.

Abused children cannot feel safe, even at times when no one is hurting them. They constantly fear that their actions may trigger an act of abuse, that a caregiver may have a bad day and arrive home angry, or that this may be the day when a parent takes drugs or drinks too much alcohol. Instead of feeling safe in their home, they may feel as though anything could happen at any time. They try hard to behave in ways that will not lead to abuse. They may or may not realize that children do not cause abuse—adults do. An abusive adult will always lash out for their own reasons regardless of what a child does or does not do.

Raising awareness of child abuse can help first responders, social workers, teachers, and other trusted adults recognize and stop it.

For many of these children, even sleeping does not provide relief. Richard Pelzer, a man who has written about the abuse he experienced as a youth, wrote, "I had perfected the ability to sleep with my eyes open and be aware of any movement within my line of vision. It was an alarm system I used when I slept. Often as a child, I was able to bring myself back into consciousness if I saw Mom cross my line of vision as she walked into my room at night. It was a safety mechanism."[1]

Pelzer's story had a happy ending. His family moved when he was a teenager, and he grew to trust his new neighbors. He told them his story. Concerned, they did some research for him and found a foster home program that accepted teenagers. Pelzer registered himself in the program. Later, as an adult, he began writing books to raise awareness about child abuse.

However, there is no happy ending for some victims of child abuse. In 2015, child abuse and neglect led to 1,670 deaths in the United States. For the survivors, though, the story does not end with the abuse. Each story continues in its own way. Some children live with the abuse until they are old enough to leave home. Some tell an adult they trust, and the trusted adult gets help for the child. Others tell an adult who does not believe them, and the abuse continues. Some become part of a child welfare investigation. In most cases, the state offers resources to the families to help them care for their children. However, some children are taken from their homes and enter foster care. Some of these children are cared for by a relative, such as a grandparent. Others go to live with foster parents who are not related to them. Still others run away from home or are legally emancipated—given freedom from their parents—by a court.

Each survivor of abuse must travel their own path toward healing. First, the abuse has to stop for good. Once this happens, survivors can begin to heal. Recovery is often slow, but it is possible for most victims.

Child Abuse in the United States

Child abuse can happen in all kinds of families. Unfortunately, many cases of child abuse are not reported. Children may live in fear and not tell anyone until they are adults. Reporting agencies do not know for sure the number of children abused every year because of the lack of reporting, but they believe thousands of children are affected by abuse.

In the Shadows

When security expert Gavin de Becker was a child, he lived in Los Angeles, California, with his physically abusive mother. One night, de Becker feared for his sister's safety. He tried to stop his mother from beating her. As he intervened, his sister ran from the house and into the street. De Becker followed. He wrote,

> We stopped at an all-night market and decided to make an anonymous call to the police ("There are two kids loitering around here"). If we didn't give our names to the police, we concluded, they wouldn't be able to take us back home. And it worked just like that. Our ride from the LAPD showed up within a few minutes and took us to jail. They could hardly put a twelve-year-old boy and a fourteen-year-old girl in with hardened criminals (though we might have felt at home), so they put us in our own cell. In the morning, we called our grandfather, who picked us up and took us home. Two kids found bruised and red-eyed and panting at three-thirty in the morning, and nobody asked us a thing. It was as if the police saw these dramas every day, and I know now that they do.[2]

As an adult, de Becker learned how common child abuse is. Now, he works with organizations and families to prevent it. As children, however, he and his sister thought their home life was normal. Many abuse survivors feel the same way until they have a chance to observe friends whose homes are quite different. Until then, they assume all families are like theirs.

It is difficult for experts to determine how many cases of child abuse occur in the United States every year. Also, government statistics on child abuse are always two or three years out of date, because the statistics are carefully reviewed before they are released to the public. In 2015, more than 4 million cases of suspected child abuse or neglect were reported to the authorities. This means that about 4 million times, someone called child welfare authorities to report that children were in danger. The number of children in danger, though, is greater than the number of calls. Generally, each call is connected with one family, which may have more than one child. In 2015, the 4 million calls concerned more than 7.2 million children. The person making the call may be a child's relative, friend, or neighbor, or even a concerned stranger. It might even be a mandated reporter—someone who is required by law to report suspected cases of child abuse. Teachers, doctors, nurses, police officers, clergy members, and social workers are all mandated reporters.

Not every phone call represents a genuine case of abuse. Of the 4 million initial phone calls reporting abuse in the United States in 2015, child welfare investigators screened-in, or decided to investigate, 1.3 million of the initial reported cases. Investigators found acts of abuse or neglect of an estimated 683,000 children. Some phone calls were false reports. Others concerned acts that did not meet the statutory definition for child abuse or neglect. These calls were screened-out, or reported to other community agencies for follow up. For example, sometimes child welfare agencies receive calls from teenagers who feel their parents are neglectful, even if their parents do provide food, clothing, and shelter. At other times, a call may be the result of a misunderstanding. For example, a neighbor may phone about children who are home alone and may not realize that an adult is actually on the premises.

Although many reported cases of child abuse do not meet the legal definition for abuse, there are also many cases of abuse that would meet the definition but are never reported. Most cases of child abuse are not reported by anyone. For this reason, experts believe the true number of cases each year is probably much higher.

AN AMERICAN TRAGEDY

"Over the past 10 years, more than 20,000 American children are believed to have been killed in their own homes by family members. That is nearly four times the number of US soldiers killed in Iraq and Afghanistan. The child maltreatment death rate in the US is triple Canada's and 11 times that of Italy. Millions of children are reported as abused and neglected every year."

—Michael Petit, founder of Every Child Matters

Quoted in "Michael Petit: Why Child Abuse is so Acute in the US," BBC, October 17, 2011. www.bbc.co.uk/news/magazine-15193530.

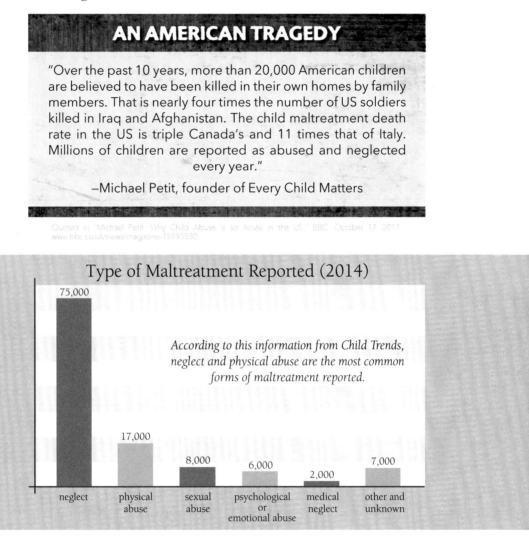

Type of Maltreatment Reported (2014)

According to this information from Child Trends, neglect and physical abuse are the most common forms of maltreatment reported.

neglect: 75,000
physical abuse: 17,000
sexual abuse: 8,000
psychological or emotional abuse: 6,000
medical neglect: 2,000
other and unknown: 7,000

Self-Reporting of Child Abuse

Since most cases of child abuse are not reported, it is difficult to compile accurate statistics about how many children are actually abused or neglected. Up until the mid-1970s, statistics on violence in American families were based on reports that were made to child welfare agencies, police reports, and reports made by emergency room staff. However, those statistics tended to underreport the actual number of abusive incidents. Most of the time, child abuse does not result in the police being called or in a child being taken to the doctor or to an emergency room. Most child abuse occurs behind closed doors, where concerned neighbors or family members are unlikely to see and report it. Most child abuse does not cause injuries that would be immediately obvious to teachers or child care workers. The statistics collected by child welfare agencies only concern those cases where children were in enough danger that the state felt it was necessary to intervene. If researchers collect only data on those cases in which outside institutions such as police, child welfare organizations, or hospitals get involved, they end up with data on only the most severe cases of child abuse.

In 1975, sociologists Richard Gelles and Murray Straus decided to try studying abuse in a new way. They wanted to have a large, national data sample, so they chose to interview people in every state. In addition, they wanted to find a way to collect data about how much abuse is really happening in American families. They did not think they could get that information just from police reports and child welfare agency statistics, so they set up a new method. They went door to door, talking to parents and caregivers in randomly chosen families nationwide. They asked parents and caregivers how they treated their children. They specifically asked about hitting children and about other acts of abuse. They also asked how adults in the family treated each other, which told them whether or not domestic violence was occurring. (In some states, causing a child to witness domestic violence is also considered an act of child abuse.)

It might seem unlikely that a person who abuses children would willingly tell a door-to-door surveyor about the abuse. However, Straus and Gelles found that a surprisingly large number of parents and caregivers did tell interviewers about acts of abuse they had committed. Almost all parents admitted to sometimes hitting their children as punishment. (Not everyone agrees with Straus and Gelles that hitting or spanking a child as punishment is a form of abuse. Spanking, also sometimes called corporal punishment, does not meet the legal definition for child abuse in most states unless it becomes severe and extreme.) The family members interviewed by Straus and Gelles also admitted committing acts of severe abuse at times. Straus and Gelles defined extreme violence as including hitting with an object such as a hairbrush or belt, kicking, punching, burning, and attacking with weapons. These sorts of acts would meet the statutory definition for physical abuse in most states.

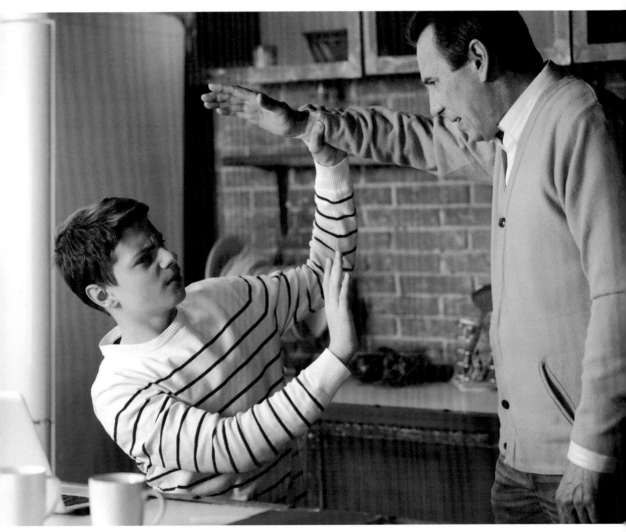

Hitting, spanking, and other physical punishment can be abusive.

Child Abuse Defined

Different people have different ideas about what constitutes child abuse. Some people consider any corporal punishment of children to be abusive. According to a poll released by the Brookings Institute in 2014, 81 percent of Americans believed that spanking a child is sometimes appropriate, while the other 19 percent believed it was never appropriate. Others only consider an action abusive if it is particularly harmful or injurious. For the state to intervene in family life, however, an act of abuse must meet the standards that are defined by law. Each state has its own laws defining what constitutes child abuse. In most states, any non-accidental physical injury to a child is considered to be physical abuse. In other states, the law provides an exception for cases of corporal punishment if it is "reasonable" and does not cause an injury.

Neglect is generally defined as deprivation of food, clothing, shelter, medical care, or supervision. Twelve states, though, make exceptions for parents who are financially unable to provide for their children. Many states have a religious exemption for parents whose religion states they cannot seek medical care, including Christian Scientists.

All states include emotional abuse in their child abuse statutes. Emotional abuse, also called psychological abuse, is defined by the American Psychological Association (APA) as "nonaccidental verbal or symbolic acts by a child's parent or caregiver that result, or have reasonable potential to result, in significant psychological harm to the child."[1] Psychological abuse can result in anxiety, depression, withdrawal, or aggressive behavior.

Although different states have different laws, each state's laws must meet standards that are set by the federal government. These standards are defined by the Child Abuse Prevention and Treatment Act (CAPTA).

1. Donald Black and Jon E. Grant, DSM-5 Guidebook: The Essential Companion to the Diagnostic and Statistical Manual of Mental Disorders, Fifth Edition. Arlington, VA: American Psychiatric Association Publishing, 2014, p. 423.

According to the data gathered by Straus and Gelles, about 2.8 million children are likely to be seriously assaulted each year in the United States.

WHEN DOES IT BECOME ABUSE?

"When does abuse become abuse? One [factor] is when the person experiences the behavior as abusive. The other is when the behavior has a negative impact on the person's capacity to function. For instance, with emotional behavior, when a kid is constantly called names or put down or belittled and that begins to have impact on her capacity to learn, or to grow, or to get on with her life, then its abuse."

—Susan Voorhees, psychologist

Quoted in Ginger Rhodes and Richard Rhodes, *Trying to Get Some Dignity: Stories of Triumph Over Childhood Abuse*. New York, NY: William Morrow and Company Inc. 1996. p. 57.

Failure to Provide: Neglect

The most common form of child abuse is neglect. This is when a parent or caretaker does not provide a child with the basic necessities, including food, clothing, shelter, medical care, education, and emotional care. More than half of child abuse cases that are investigated by Child Protective Services involve neglect. Neglect can be defined differently in different states. There are many kinds of neglect that fall within these categories.

Many neglect cases involve parents leaving their children unsupervised, often because the parents do not have child care available when they are working. Another common form of neglect is to expose children to illegal drugs. When a child's mother is a drug user, she may expose her child to drugs unintentionally by taking drugs while she is pregnant or breastfeeding. In 14 states and Washington, D.C., prenatal, or pre-birth, exposure to drugs constitutes child abuse, and in 19 states and Washington, D.C., there are reporting procedures for newborn babies who show evidence of having been exposed to drugs or alcohol while in the womb. A 2013 study that reviewed national information between 1973 and 2005 showed 413 cases against pregnant women, 84 percent of which were drug-related offenses. Older children may also be affected by their parents' drug use. In 2016, a 16-year-old boy died of an overdose of heroin given to him by his mother. She later told police she wanted to be the "cool weekend mom" and gave her son drugs.

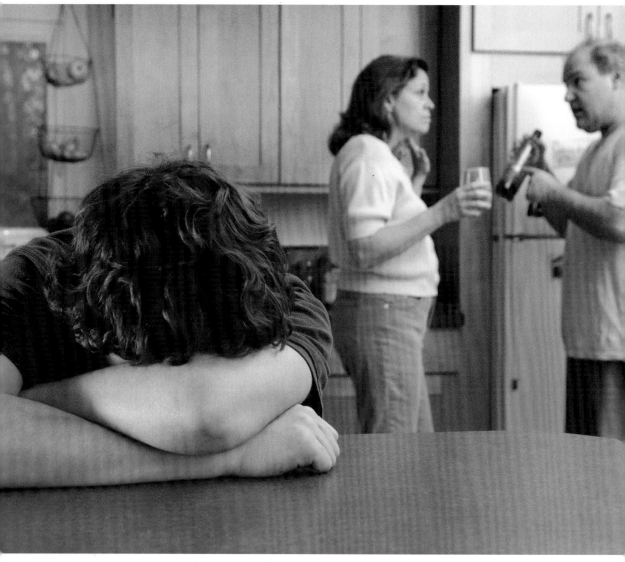

Parents with drug or alcohol dependencies often neglect their children.

However, there are also many neglect cases based on failure to feed and clothe children, failure to provide them with needed medical care, or failure to provide them with adequate shelter. Former New York social worker Marc Parent wrote about handling one such case. He received the following report:

> Mother lives alone with her five children—aged 2 yrs to 7 yrs. There is no furniture in the home. Children sleep on the floor and are frequently seen "running wild" in the hallways. The building is very run-down and there are drug dealers on every floor. The children are often seen naked and unsupervised. Unknown if there is food in the home now. Mother just had a baby and the infant appears to be thin and weak.[3]

In a case like this, child protection workers visit the home. They try to determine whether or not there is food in the house, whether or not the children have been fed regularly, whether they have been provided with clothing, and whether they are supervised. They must assess whether the parent is willing and able to care for the children in question. In many cases, parents and caregivers are trying their best to provide for their children. Sometimes, they are overwhelmed by financial problems or the stress of caring for several children at once. In these cases, child protection workers may be able to direct the family to community resources that can help. For example, they could help a single mother apply for aid from the Women, Infants, and Children (WIC) program. WIC is a federal program that gives money to states to provide food for children under the age of five and their mothers.

In some cases, neglect is caused by mental illness. While working in New York City, Parent also received this report:

> Mother believes she and her children are under a hex. Mother is not feeding children because she is afraid of the food. The children are hungry now. Mother is behaving strangely. She is not answering the phone and will not open the door for anyone. Last week Mother reported seeing "strange men" outside of her apartment window. Mother lives on the 16th floor. There are bizarre sounds coming from the apartment and it is believed that the children are at risk.[4]

When he visited this apartment, Parent and his partner found a single mother who genuinely loved and cared for her children but who was mentally ill. As the social workers talked with her, they discovered that she believed a hex would cause any food she brought into the house to become embedded with shards of glass if it was not eaten right away. She was afraid to feed her children because she thought shards of glass were in the food. In this case, child protection workers took temporary custody of the children, hoping that the children could be reunited with their mother after her mental illness was treated.

Harm to the Body: Physical Abuse

Neglect can take a physical toll on children. It may leave them malnourished, for example, and can cause developmental delays. However, in cases of neglect, parents or caregivers may not actually intend to harm their children. They may simply fail to care for them. They may not have enough money to buy food or clothes. They may be mentally ill. They may be addicted to alcohol or drugs, or they may not understand how to care for a very young child.

Nearly one-third of child abuse cases, however, involve harm that was done to a child deliberately. In most states, a deliberate, non-accidental injury to a child is considered physical abuse. Thirty-six states also include threats of harm in their definitions for physical abuse. In addition, these states include, as part of their physical abuse definition, taking actions that risk harming a child, even if the child was not actually harmed. For example, forcing a child to sit on the windowsill of a 20-story building is child abuse, even if the child does not fall and is not physically harmed. (Some states classify this type of act as child endangerment.)

Sexual acts forced on a child are always considered abusive as well, even if they do not result in a visible injury. Sexual abuse by a related caretaker or parent is also called incest. Incest can happen to children of all ages and of any sex. According to survivor Barbara Hamilton, "The emotional essence of incest is to feel oneself becoming spoiled to the core and powerless to stop it."[5] Children who are sexually abused may feel ashamed and unable to talk about the abuse. They may also wrongly believe, like other abused children do, that they were responsible for causing the abuse.

Physical abuse is less common than neglect, but it is easier for mandated child abuse reporters, such as doctors and nurses, to spot. Doctors and nurses become concerned about physical abuse when they see a child who has a pattern of injuries that have occurred regularly over a period of time. For example, they may see bruises or burns on different parts of the body, all in different stages of healing. When multiple injuries are all in different stages of healing, a doctor can figure out that the injuries occurred on several different occasions, not all at once.

Doctors can also recognize certain kinds of injuries as more likely than others to be the result of physical abuse. Children often injure themselves in the course of everyday life. However, an injury caused by a fall or by playing sports will generally be located in a part of the body that is frequently exposed and not well protected. For example, typical childhood injuries might be located on the shins, knees, hands, elbows, nose, or forehead. Doctors are more suspicious if they see bruises on the buttocks, thighs, torso, ears, or neck. They suspect child abuse if they see bruises shaped like a hand, belt buckle, electrical cord loop, or other object. Doctors also become suspicious if they find bruises on babies who have not yet learned to walk. Babies that young are unlikely to hurt themselves accidentally.

One type of physical abuse many doctors have become experts at recognizing is shaken baby syndrome. Shaken baby syndrome is damage to a baby that is caused by shaking the baby. Babies who have been shaken tend to appear in the emergency room with bleeding inside their brains and eyes. They often have broken ribs as well. Babies with shaken baby syndrome are often too young to walk or crawl. They are unlikely to have broken their own ribs or to have shaken their own heads hard enough to cause internal bleeding, so emergency room workers can quickly figure out what must have happened.

For example, in 2017, doctors at St. John's Hospital emergency room in Springfield, Illinois, alerted police that a five-month-old was suffering from shaken baby syndrome. The

Medical professionals are often able to identify physical abuse by taking into account the age of the child and the patterns or shapes of injuries such as bruises.

baby had been brought to the hospital because of seizure-like symptoms and difficulty breathing. Doctors found evidence of bleeding in the brain and of possibly older injuries that had healed. The baby's mother, 18-year-old Kenisha Q. Ray, admitted that she had shaken the child vigorously. She also admitted that she had previously shaken the child four or five times. Ray was arrested and charged with aggravated battery in the abuse of her child.

False Witness?

Not all accusations of child abuse turn out to be true. In 2015, child welfare agencies received more than 4 million calls reporting possible cases of child abuse or neglect. Of the original 4 million calls, only about 18 percent were found to concern verifiable cases of child abuse.

Every year, there are a few cases that are verified at first but are later discovered not to be true. In 2015, two Maryland siblings, ages 10 and 6, were picked up by police for walking alone on a main road. A neighbor saw the children and called Child Protective Services. When the parents were notified, they explained that the children knew the neighborhood and were allowed to walk to and from the playground. The family was held for questioning for five hours, and the parents were charged with neglect. After an investigation, the state ruled the parents had not been neglectful and dropped the charges. The case led to the state reviewing and updating its definitions of parental neglect.

Damage to the Mind: Emotional Abuse

When people think about child abuse, they generally think about cases involving shaken baby syndrome or other forms of physical abuse or neglect. However, most states also include emotional abuse in their child abuse laws. Emotional abuse means failing to meet a child's emotional needs or causing a child to experience psychological damage. All forms of child abuse cause emotional and psychological damage. However, some children are abused emotionally without having ever been injured physically.

What is emotional abuse? According to Patricia Leiby, "The child who constantly hears how dumb he is, or that he can't do [anything], is emotionally abused."[6] However, this is only one method abusers use. Insulting a child consistently, denying the abuse happened to make the child question their reality, destroying something the child loves, telling siblings one is better than the others, being overly controlling, scaring the child on purpose, and giving a child the silent treatment are all forms of emotional abuse. However, for emotional abuse to reach a point that would warrant intervention by state authorities, it must fall within the definition included in the laws of the state. Most state laws define it as psychological or emotional damage that leads to the development of a mental disorder such as anxiety or depression.

According to legal scholar J. Robert Shull, psychological abuse can consist of any "imaginative cruelty"[7] that does not involve physical injury or sexual abuse. Imaginative cruelty does not necessarily mean thinking of more creative but hurtful things to say to a child. It could also involve non-injurious physical acts. For example, in Lancaster, Pennsylvania, Elsa Speller locked her 13-year-old daughter in a closet for 17 hours. She provided a bucket for a toilet but gave the girl no food or water. Patricia Muncy of La Grande, Oregon, chained her 13-year-old daughter to a tree for two days.

Psychological injury can also be caused by a pattern of verbally belittling a child. Parents may occasionally, or even regularly, criticize their children without it being considered child abuse; the key difference is that with abuse, the criticism is often untrue and meant to be hurtful. Abuse can also mean damaging a child's personal possessions or humiliating the child in front of friends, or it could involve threatening a child's pet or deliberately hurting a pet while forcing the child to watch. In families that are experiencing domestic violence or spousal abuse, a child might be emotionally injured by being forced to watch one of their parents being hurt or threatened.

Most child abuse experts consider repeated emotional abuse to be far more damaging—and far more common—than isolated physical abuse. Psychologists James Garbarino, Edna Guttman, and Janis Wilson Seeley wrote, "Children are resilient, and they can handle parents' normal emotional ebb and flow; what most children typically cannot handle is a pervasive pattern of destructive emotions or extreme outbursts that threaten their world. Isolated trauma is not nearly so threatening as repeated emotional assault."[8]

In other words, it is easier for children to recover from the physical damage of an assault that occurs on rare occasions than it is for them to live with constant belittling, name-calling, and intimidation. Unfortunately, many abused children must recover from both.

CHAPTER 2

Abuse at Any Age

Child abuse can occur in any type of home. It occurs in wealthy families, middle-class families, and poor families. Abuse is committed by people of every race, sex, ethnicity, religion, and sexual orientation. Child abuse can be committed by caregivers with drug or alcohol problems as well as by sober parents. Victims and perpetrators look like anyone else.

It Happens Everywhere

"My mother drank heavily," remembered Denise, a child abuse survivor who grew up to be an attorney. "I've never been sure whether it was deliberate, or whether she was just so blind drunk she didn't realize what she was doing, but she burned me with a lit cigarette. And I can still remember that pain."[9]

Denise's mother was an alcoholic. Two-year-old Benjamin Metz-Johnson's mother, Carrie Metz, was addicted to a different substance: heroin. She was taking methadone, a prescription drug used to wean addicts off heroin. Metz had her medication bottle on the counter of her kitchen. In January 2007, Benjamin grabbed the cup containing methadone, which is extremely toxic for young children, from Metz's counter. Metz later testified that she did not believe Benjamin had ingested any of the methadone, so she did not take him to a doctor. A few hours later, he turned blue and stopped breathing, and he died. Metz was charged and convicted of child neglect and sentenced to six years in prison.

These two stories could have come from any family in any home in America. Denise grew up in a wealthy, two-parent family in a suburb of Boston. Benjamin was the son of a struggling single mother in Kenosha, Wisconsin. People with an addiction to drugs or alcohol, such as Denise's and Benjamin's mothers, are three times more likely than the average person to abuse a child and four times more likely to neglect one. However, many children are also abused by adults who do not drink or take drugs, and there are many people with addictions who do not abuse their children.

A Familiar Perpetrator

Perpetrator is a term used by law enforcement agencies to describe the person who committed a crime or an act of wrongdoing. In some ways, it is correct to say that there is no typical case of child abuse. Each family is different, each child is different, and each caregiver is different. However, even though child abuse occurs in all kinds of families, child welfare authorities see certain trends in the cases in which they are asked to intervene.

Most perpetrators of child abuse and neglect are in their mid-20s but had their first child before the age of 18. Most do not have a high school diploma and have not completed any higher education, such as college or vocational school. Most are living at or below the poverty level. Frequently, perpetrators of abuse and neglect are depressed and have difficulty coping with stress in their lives. Many child abusers were abused themselves as children. A history that includes being the victim of abuse puts a person at a very slightly increased chance of abusing children themselves. However, most survivors of child abuse do not grow up to become child abusers—most cannot imagine subjecting other children to the experiences that they endured.

Almost all perpetrators of child abuse and neglect have one thing in common—they are people who are responsible for caring for and supervising children. In 2015, more than 78 percent of perpetrators of child abuse and neglect were the parents of the victims. About 13 percent were nonparent caretakers, such as daycare providers, babysitters, and relatives. Another 2.8 percent were abused by unknown perpetrators. In those cases, children were unable or unwilling to identify their abusers, and investigators were not able to identify the perpetrators.

Men and women are equally likely to commit acts of child abuse and neglect. However, the type of abuse they commit varies by sex. Neglect is generally committed by mothers, while violence and physical abuse are most commonly committed by fathers or by male caretakers.

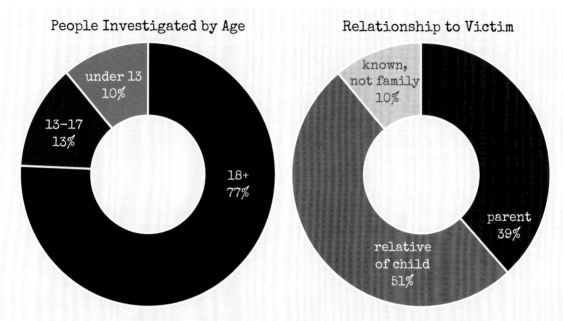

As this information from the National Children's Alliance shows, perpetrators of child abuse are often more than 18 years old and a relative of the child.

Mental Illness and Child Abuse

Children in homes where parents have certain characteristics are more likely to be abused or neglected. Parents who have drug or alcohol dependencies, mental illness, or experience domestic abuse are more likely to abuse their children.

A parent or caregiver does not have to be mentally ill to commit an act of child abuse. Most commonly, a child abuser is angry, frustrated, overwhelmed, or otherwise overcome with negative emotions. However, in some cases, parents are mentally ill. These parents may commit acts of abuse without fully realizing what they are doing. For example, in 2016, a woman in South Carolina killed her two children and attempted to kill her husband in their sleep. When questioned, she stated that she wanted the family to be reincarnated in another, better world.

Children's Reactions

In 2016, Katlyn Marin was sentenced to 45 years to life in prison for murdering her daughter, Brielle. Marin had five children, and they lived with severe abuse for years. Despite the efforts of local police and child protection workers, the children were returned to their mother time and again until Brielle was killed. At Marin's sentencing, a state prosecutor read a letter from one of Marin's sons, which said, "I miss Brielle's face, pretty smile and playing. It's still hard to talk about what happened and I still feel sad. Do you care about how you hurt us?"[1]

1. Quoted in Allie Morris, "Fatal flaws–Part 1 of 4: Inside the Last Year of Brielle Gage's life," Concord Monitor, April 8, 2017, www.concordmonitor.com/division-for-children-youth-and-families-DCYF-brielle-gage-9060589.

Most parents who have mental disorders do not abuse their children. However, mental illness increases a parent's risk of committing abuse or neglect. The risk is highest in parents who have been diagnosed with a severe mental illness, such as schizophrenia or major depression. Schizophrenia, for example, can cause a person to have hallucinations and delusions and to hear voices. It can make parents confused about their surroundings or about how best to keep their children safe, even if they genuinely love and care for their children. Depression, in contrast, may make parents more likely to neglect their children, simply by making it harder for parents to function normally. Some depressed parents find it difficult even to get out of bed in the morning. It is hard for them, therefore, to deal with feeding and caring for a young child.

Researchers believe that people with mental disorders can still be good parents to their children. For some people, depression does not affect their parenting abilities, but other parents may need extra support. For example, they may need medication or therapy. Many need financial support, especially to pay for health care, and they may have an even greater need than many other parents do for financial assistance to help them pay for child care and housing.

Child abuse as neglect can happen when a parent refuses to prevent the abuse. Although only one parent is physically abusing the child in many abusive situations, the other parent neglects to help the child by stopping the abuse.

Victims of Neglect

Perpetrators of neglect may believe they are very different from people who physically abuse children. However, neglect can be just as hard on a child as physical abuse. For example, on August 13, 2008, a neighbor reported hearing screaming coming from the home of Jon Pomeroy and Rebecca Long in Carnation, Washington. A sheriff's deputy visited and found Pomeroy's 14-year-old daughter near death from malnutrition. Pomeroy and Long had restricted her to half a cup of water per day. At night, they made her sleep in their bedroom and slid a heavy dresser in front of the door to prevent her from leaving. Pomeroy's daughter had a history of sneaking out of her bedroom at night to drink out of the toilet bowl, because she was afraid her parents would hear the water running if she used the faucet.

When she was found, Pomeroy's daughter was badly dehydrated and emaciated. She was 4 feet 7 inches (1.4 m) tall and weighed 48 pounds (22 kg). Her teeth were beginning to fall out from malnutrition. The sheriff's deputy who found her rushed her to Seattle Children's Hospital, where she remained for two weeks.

Gregory Jones and Jessica Lee Lovell of Jackson, Mississippi, had two children, a 5-month-old and a 16-month-old. Both had been born prematurely and needed to see a doctor regularly. When Jones and Lovell stopped taking their children to their doctor, he feared for the children's lives. He phoned the police and reported that the children might be in danger. When child protection investigators arrived at their home, they discovered that the children were badly malnourished and dehydrated. Investigators called an ambulance and took the children to the hospital. Jones and Lovell were charged with child endangerment for neglecting to feed their children.

Child neglect can lead to malnourishment and dehydration.

Cases of neglect, such as those of Pomeroy and Long or Jones and Lovell, are the most common type of child abuse in the United States. Neglect is three times more common than physical abuse.

Children are much more likely to be neglected if they are living in poverty. According to researchers at the National Center for Children in Poverty, nearly 15 million American children were living in poverty in 2017. Why are children living in poverty more likely to be neglected? Sometimes parents do not have the resources they need to take adequate care of their children. A common example is a single mother of a four-year-old and a six-year-old who works the night shift. Having no child care, she may tuck her children into bed at night and go to work, hoping for the best. However, leaving young children without adequate supervision is a form of neglect.

Even though poverty increases a child's chances of being abused, most impoverished parents and caregivers do not neglect the children in their care. Out of the nearly 15 million children living in poverty in the United States in 2017, fewer than 1 million were abused or neglected, and not all of those abuse and neglect victims came from poor families.

POVERTY, MENTAL HEALTH, AND NEGLECT

"The Urban Institute found that 11 percent of infants living in poverty have a mother suffering from severe depression. Fifty-five percent of all infants living in poverty are being raised by mothers with some form of depression ... Evidence suggests that depression can interfere with parenting, potentially leading to poor child development—setbacks that are particularly devastating during infancy. Compared with their peers who are living in poverty with nondepressed mothers, infants living in poverty with severely depressed mothers are more likely to have mothers who also struggle with domestic violence and substance abuse, and who report being only in fair health."
—Maren K. Dale, staff attorney at U.S. Court of Appeals for the Eleventh Circuit

Maren K. Dale, "Addressing the Underlying Issue of Poverty in Child-Neglect Cases," April 10, 2014.
apps.americanbar.org/litigation/committees/childrights/content/articles/spring2014-0414-address-
ing-underlying-issue-poverty-child-neglect-cases.html.

Victims of Physical Abuse

At about 9:20 p.m. on a Sunday evening in August 2008, Michael Below, a new father in West Bend, Wisconsin, became frustrated with his two-month-old daughter. She would not stop crying, and her mother was at work. Later, Below told investigators that he picked the baby up by her feet and began banging her head against her diaper-changing table. Investigators noted, "On a scale of one to 10, 10 being the hardest, defendant hit [the baby's] head on the changing table about eight or nine."[10]

Pretending that nothing was wrong, Below took the baby with him when he went to pick up her mother from work at 10 p.m. However, the baby was breathing strangely, and her mother became frightened. She called an ambulance. On admission at Children's Hospital of Wisconsin, the baby was found to have severe brain injuries, bleeding in her eyes, a skull fracture, and brain swelling. Those injuries had occurred that evening, but doctors also found older injuries: broken ribs and an older area of bleeding in her brain.

When investigators asked Below what had happened, he told them he was under a lot of stress. He was worried about his finances. Investigators noted in their report that "he does not know what got over him, that he just lost control and was frustrated."[11]

Below's story is an example of the second most common type of child abuse—physical abuse. Unlike neglect, which is associated more with families living in poverty, physical abuse is just as likely to occur in wealthy families as it is in poor families. However, it is slightly more common in families that have experienced a divorce, separation, and remarriage. The children who are most at risk for physical abuse are the very young, especially children who are under the age of four. Teens are the next most commonly abused age group, but children ages four to twelve are also frequently abused. Boys are more likely to be beaten, while girls are more likely to be sexually assaulted.

The most at-risk children are those who are especially hard to care for. This group includes, for example, children who had low birth weights or who were premature, such as Jones and

Lovell's children. It also includes children who are physically disabled or developmentally delayed. It is especially easy for an abuser to overpower a child who is unusually small, weak, or disabled. When these children grow older and stronger, the abuse sometimes decreases because the abuser is afraid of being hit back. As babies, though, children do not hit back. They can cry, but crying may trigger some caregivers to become angry and violent.

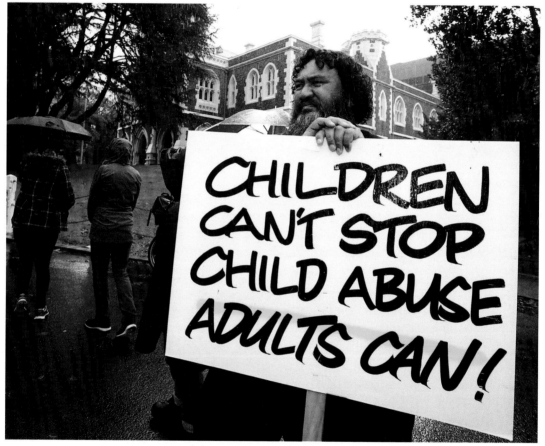

Caring adults can advocate for child abuse victims.

Some child welfare advocates find that children in families with only one or two children are more at risk than children in larger families. This may be because older children may step in to try to protect younger children from abuse. In some cases, older children will stand between a caregiver and a younger sibling, trying to protect the younger sibling. More often, older children simply step in and help with child care. As a result, the younger children in the family spend less time with a parent who might abuse them. This may help keep younger children in the family safe, but it also forces older children to care for children before they have become adults themselves.

Unaccompanied Youth

Child abuse is one of the most common reasons why children end up living on the street, homeless. These children are referred to as unaccompanied youth. They may have run away from home or been kicked out of their homes. Between 1.6 million and 2.8 million youth run away from their homes every year. A study of runaway youth that examined data over 15 years found that verbal, physical, and sexual abuse at home corresponded with higher runaway rates. Around 17 percent of children who run away from home say they left in order to escape physical abuse at home. Another study, from 1998, put the rate of physical abuse before leaving home at 43 percent.

"Throwaway" children are children whose families have thrown them out. Among throwaway children, the incidence of abuse and neglect is even higher than it is among runaways. A survey of youth in shelters found that 50 percent of throwaway children were told to leave by their parents or their parents did not try to stop them from leaving.

There are a number of risk factors for unaccompanied youth. Children who are Latinx, have been in foster care, or who do not identify as heterosexual are more likely to run away or be thrown out of the house.

Children who are runaways or throwaways are at higher risk for adverse life events. These children, alone on the streets, are more likely to be taken advantage of, to be trafficked for sex, and to develop drug and alcohol dependencies.

Fatal Abuse

In most cases, child abuse is not fatal. Unfortunately, though, sometimes children do die from abuse. Sometimes, they die from injuries caused by physical abuse. They may also die from neglect if they are extremely malnourished or have been denied medical care. In rare cases, they can die from what would normally be considered a kind of emotional abuse—being confined to a small area. In 2008, 16-year-old Calista Springer of Centreville, Michigan, died in a house fire. Her parents had chained her to her bed—a form of emotional abuse. When her house caught on fire, she was unable to escape and died in the blaze. Springer's mother later pleaded no contest to charges of child neglect, and Springer's sisters were taken from the family and placed in the care of relatives.

According to the National Child Abuse and Neglect Data System, in 2015, authorities were aware of 1,670 children in the United States who died as a result of injuries caused by abuse. Experts believe, though, that more than half of all fatalities caused by child abuse are classified as accidents rather than abuse. In the United States, 2.25 children out of every 100,000 die each year from physical abuse.

Homicide cases are not particularly different from other child abuse cases, except that they involve a death. The perpetrators of homicide cases share the same characteristics as the perpetrators of nonfatal abuse. As in other child abuse cases, the perpetrators of child homicides are generally the parent or caregiver—80 percent of child homicides involve at least one parent.

Sometimes, the perpetrator of a homicide is someone that most people would not think of, such as a sibling. For example, New York City social worker Marc Parent was called to investigate a case that was expected to end in a fatality. A five-year-old boy was in a coma, and his four-year-old brother had been hospitalized as well. At first, the social workers believed the children's mother or aunt was responsible for the injuries. However, as they investigated, they realized that the children's nine-year-old babysitter, their cousin, had beaten them.

Abusive Head Trauma, or Shaken Babies

Every year, between 1,000 and 3,000 children in the United States are killed or injured by caregivers who become frustrated with the demands of baby care and shake their babies. The resulting injuries are termed shaken baby syndrome or abusive head trauma. According to the National Center on Shaken Baby Syndrome, crying is the number-one trigger for adults who shake children. Most of these babies are under six months old, and about 25 percent of shaken babies die from their injuries. It only takes a few seconds of violent shaking to permanently injure or kill a baby.

Eighty percent of babies who survive shaking have permanent damage, sometimes becoming disabled. They may have severe brain damage and may develop cerebral palsy or become mentally disabled. Some children are so seriously injured that they are never able to breathe on their own. They must depend on a respirator. Some babies are left blind or unable to feel touch. These children require constant medical attention. Some babies do survive shaking and go on to lead relatively normal lives. Even in these cases, though, children often have behavior problems. They may have a hard time controlling sudden impulses and find it difficult to organize their work or to concentrate in school.

Although the perpetrators of child abuse homicides often match the perpetrators of other forms of child abuse, the victims are slightly different. Nonfatal child abuse tends to target very young children and teenagers, but fatal child abuse predominantly affects very young children. Young children are more vulnerable to violence than older children, and they may die from acts that would not kill an older child.

Babies and preschoolers are at the highest risk for being killed by their parents or caretakers. More than 74 percent of abuse fatalities were children under the age of three. When fatal abuse happens, it often happens during the first few weeks of the child's life. Sometimes, newborns are killed by their mothers. At other times, mothers abandon babies in public places, where they may freeze or starve to death before a rescue occurs.

Preschool children, on the other hand, are more often killed when their parents or caretakers try to control their behavior. They may also be killed in situations where parents or caregivers become angry in response to normal preschool-aged behavior, such as crying, hitting, getting dirty, or not adapting to toilet training. Parents may react to such behavior by throwing the child against a hard surface or by hitting or smothering the

For children who have lived in an abusive situation, finding a safe environment is essential.

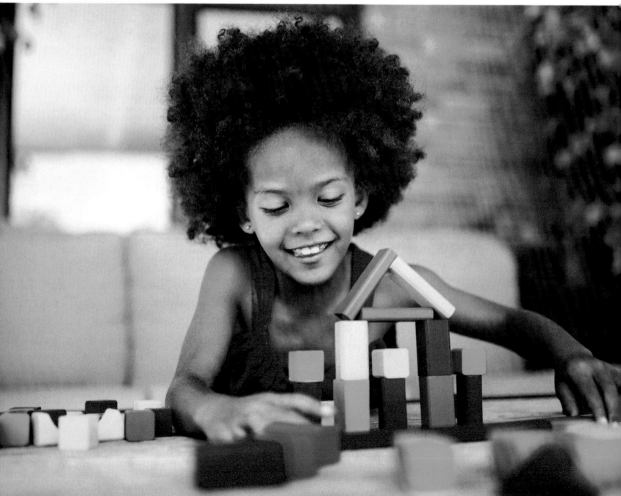

child. They may not intend to kill the child but may not realize how fragile a very young child can be.

To children and adults who have not had to live with abuse or neglect, stories of abused children sound horrific. However, children who live through abuse may not realize that there is anything unusual about their family lives. To them, abuse and neglect are a normal condition of everyday life. They may not mention the abuse to friends or caring adults. They may feel afraid that they will not be believed, they may have been wrongly told by their abusers that the abuse is their own fault, or their abuser may have threatened further abuse if they tell someone.

For children to recover from this kind of life, they need something more than a safe place to live and grow. They need an environment in which they are encouraged to develop their own interests and begin to believe that they deserve to be happy. Frequently, child welfare workers are able to work with a child's family to help the family become a unit that allows children to thrive and be happy. At other times, the original family is so unsafe that children must be placed with another family. Either way, the state monitors the children to make sure that they are well cared for and remain safe.

Investigating Child Abuse

Investigating abuse starts with making a report. Often, a report of child abuse comes from a child's teachers, neighbors, doctors, or family members. After potential abuse is reported to authorities, the next step is to investigate. This generally means speaking with a child's parents or caregivers. It may seem unbelievable, but some abusers do not think they are doing anything wrong and will tell investigators the truth about their own abusive behaviors.

In October 2007, a five-year-old from Mesa, Arizona, told her teacher that her father and stepmother had been beating her. The teacher took the girl to the school nurse, who documented nearly 100 bruises on the girl's back, legs, arms, buttocks, and chest. Teachers and school nurses are required to report cases of suspected child abuse, so they phoned the Mesa police.

Mesa police officers went to the girl's home and interviewed her parents. Her father, Ezra Hazell, explained that he beat her if she was disobedient or if she did not do her homework. He told police that he and Kristie Hazell, the girl's stepmother, would have their five-year-old hold a push-up position. He said they would put a book on the floor in front of her, and if she did not pay attention to the book or did not understand a particular word, they would beat her several times with a belt. Ezra Hazell also told investigators that he sometimes beat his daughter with a computer cord. The Mesa police investigators were appalled by Hazell's story. Hazell and his wife were arrested, and their children were placed in the care of relatives.

Police can help uncover child abuse.

Eventually, Ezra Hazell was sentenced to eight months in jail and ten years of probation. Kristie Hazell was sentenced to ten years of probation.

Mandatory Reporting

In the Hazell case, the child reported her own abuse. However, child welfare agencies accept reports of child abuse from anyone. A neighbor, a family member, or a child's friend can pick up the phone and call a child abuse hotline. An abused child can even call on their own behalf. For example, anyone can call the Childhelp National Child Abuse Hotline, which is staffed seven days a week, twenty-four hours a day. They could also call the local department of children and family services or the police.

However, although anyone can report abuse, people who work in certain jobs are required to report abuse. They do not have to be certain that abuse occurred; they only have to suspect it. People who are required by law to report suspected abuse are called mandated reporters. The Hazell case was reported when the abused girl told her story to two mandated reporters—her teacher and the school nurse. Doctors, dentists, social workers, counselors, law enforcement officers, and child care providers are also mandated reporters. Mandated reporters must report suspected child abuse right away by making a phone call. Then, they are required to follow up within a day with a written report.

If a mandated reporter does not follow through on making a report when they suspect a child is being abused or neglected, they may face a penalty under the law. Currently, 48 states and Washington, D.C., have penalties in place for a mandated reporter who fails to report the suspected abuse. For example, a person who fails to make a report in Florida can be charged with a felony. In New York, they can be charged with a Class A misdemeanor, receive criminal penalties, and even be sued in a civil court for any harm caused by their failure to make a report.

When child welfare agencies receive a report of abuse, they must assess it. This means that they must decide whether

Mandated reporters include teachers, doctors, and other professionals who work with children.

the report is likely to concern a case of child abuse or not. It also means they must determine whether or not they have enough information to find out more. For example, a community member might report abuse that was observed in the grocery store or on a bus or train. However, child welfare investigators may not have enough information to follow up on this kind of report. They may not have names or addresses, for example. Investigators also must screen out calls that do not have anything to do with child abuse. For example, they may get phone calls from people who disagree with a parent's choices about how late to let a teenager stay out at night, or they may get phone calls from people who are concerned about a child with a drug addiction. In response to that kind of call, investigators would refer the caller to a community agency that offers substance abuse or rehabilitation programs.

A Danger to Children

In the end, investigators generally screen out about one-third of reports of child abuse. They follow up on the other two-thirds of abuse reports. Because child welfare agencies have limited staff, though, they cannot always follow up right away. Instead, they try to focus on the cases in which a child is thought to be in immediate danger. Of course, it is impossible for investigators to know, prior to conducting an investigation, which children are actually in immediate danger.

To help them assess the danger, investigators consider the elements of abuse mentioned by the original caller. If the caller said that the child had many injuries and that all the injuries were different (for example, a burn, bruises, and a broken bone), or if the injuries were all to the face and head, investigators feel they should respond more quickly. Likewise, if a child is thought to be home alone, is thought to be in need of immediate medical attention, or is alleged to be badly malnourished, child protection workers try to go to the scene immediately. Investigators also respond immediately if they hear that a caregiver is behaving bizarrely or is under the influence of drugs or alcohol.

In a Child's Own Words

Once investigators determine that a report is real and should be investigated, they must interview the child who is alleged to have been abused. The investigators' first priority at this point is still to find out if the child is in any immediate danger, but they must also try to reassure the child. Counselor Connie Carnes noted, "It is very important for the interviewer … to stay attuned to the child's psychological state during the interview. Because the last thing we would want to do is to retraumatize the child by the way that we interview them."[12]

It is not always easy for investigators to convince children to talk to them. Children may love their parents and caregivers deeply even if they are being abused or neglected. They generally do not want to say anything critical about their parents, relatives, or other caregivers. Sometimes, they are afraid that they will get in trouble if they say anything. Dave Pelzer, the brother of Richard Pelzer and author of the book *A Child Called "It,"* told his teacher, Miss Moss, and his school principal, Mr. Hansen. He remembered being interviewed about his mother's abuse:

> The police officer explains why Mr. Hansen called him. I can feel myself shrink into the chair. The officer asks that I tell him about Mother. I shake my head no. Too many people already know the secret, and I know she'll find out. A soft voice calms me. I think it's Miss Moss. She tells me it's all right. I take a deep breath, wring my hands and reluctantly tell them about Mother and me. Then the nurse has me stand up and show the policeman the scar on my chest. Without hesitation, I tell them it was an accident; which it was—Mother never meant to stab me.[13]

Investigators also interview the child's parents or guardians, as well as the person or persons who are thought to have committed the abuse. Sometimes, parents who have physically abused their kids understand that what they did was wrong and illegal. They try to cover it up by lying; they may say that the child fell or that the injuries came from playing sports. Other parents may not believe corporal punishment is abuse. These parents may be very honest with investigators, as Ezra Hazell was. They may tell investigators exactly what they did and come up with a reason why they thought their actions were justified by the child's behavior.

While investigators interview the parents or caregivers and the children, they also assess the condition of the family home. They try to determine whether the home is a safe environment and take time to interview friends and neighbors who know the family. Investigators also review any paperwork connected with the family. They find out if there have been prior allegations of child abuse or neglect. They review each child's medical history and any criminal history the parents or caregivers may have. They also review school files for each child in the family.

In the end, investigators will classify each case of potential child abuse as substantiated or unsubstantiated. A substantiated case is one in which most of the evidence suggests that abuse probably did occur. Investigators can classify a case as substantiated even if they do not have enough evidence to convict an abuser in court. If they classify the case as unsubstantiated, it means they could not find enough evidence to prove that abuse really occurred. In 2015, about 18 percent of child abuse reports in the United States were found to be substantiated.

INTERVIEWING VICTIMS OF TRAUMA

"Children who have been victims of maltreatment or were witnesses to violent crime often react uniquely to their experiences ... trauma symptoms may interfere with a child's ability or willingness to report information about violent incidents ... Interviewers and those involved in investigating child abuse may need to modify their expectations of what a traumatized child is able to report. They should not attempt to force a disclosure or continue an interview when a child becomes overly distressed, which may revictimize the child."
—Office of Juvenile Justice and Delinquency Prevention team of the U.S. Department of Justice

Chris Newlin, Linda Cordisco Steele, Andra Chamberlin, et al., "Child Forensic Interviewing: Best Practices," Juvenile Justice Bulletin, September 2015, p. 3. www.ojjdp.gov/pubs/248749.pdf.

Problems with False Reporting

Some critics of the child welfare system argue that children are often removed without due process of law. Due process is a legal term that means an accused person is not assumed to be guilty but instead must have the opportunity to defend themselves by presenting evidence and witnesses in court. Some parents argue that they have been subjected to a full-scale children's services investigation just on the basis of a phone call from a neighbor. These parents argue that even if children are not removed from the home, parents are still exposed to the embarrassment of having investigators ask family members, friends, neighbors, and teachers about the possibility of abuse.

Virginia mother Cari Clark said her name was listed on the Virginia state registry of child abusers and neglectors simply because her neighbor called the state to report that one of Clark's children was walking unsupervised in the neighborhood. "It's not like calling a cop when there's a noisy party," Clark explained. "They don't just send someone around to say hey, cool it. It's a full-scale investigation that can turn a family's life inside out."[1]

1. Quoted in David Wagner, "Child Removal Lacks Due Process," *Insight on the News*, November 24, 1997, p. 22.

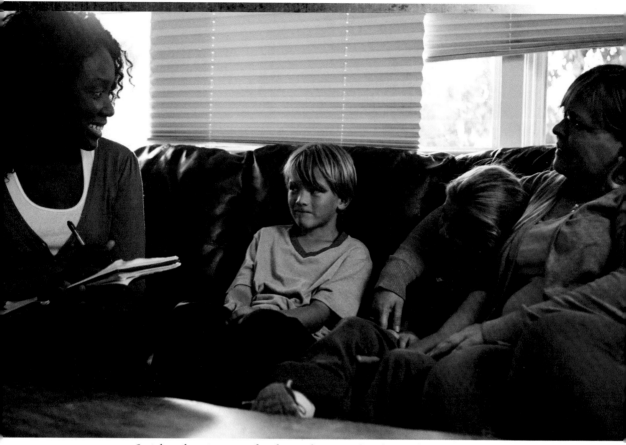

Social workers interview families to determine how best to help a child.

A SAFE HOME IN FOSTER CARE

"All children need safe, permanent families that love, nurture, protect, and guide them ... Children in foster care cannot count on things that all children should be able to take for granted—that they have constant, loving parents; that their home will always be their home; that their brothers and sisters will always be near; and that their neighborhoods and schools are familiar places."
–William Gray, formerly of Pew Commission on Children in Foster Care

Pew Commission on Children in Foster Care, "Fostering the Future: Safety, Permanence and Well-Being for Children in Foster Care," accessed September 12, 2017, p. 9. www.pewtrusts.org/~/media/legacy/uploadedfiles/phg/content_level_pages/reports/0012pdf.pdf.

Families in Trouble

In many cases, investigators find families who may not have abused or neglected their children but whom the investigators think are at risk for abuse or neglect. For example, sometimes a doctor suspects, but is not certain, that a child is being neglected. The child might not be as tall or weigh as much as is considered typical for their age, but that alone would not prove neglect. Some children are naturally small or thin. Also, some parents feed a child less because of poverty but provide as much food as they can with the financial resources that they have. If parents are trying their best to take care of their children but fail to do so only because of poverty, many states will grant them an exception to charges of neglect. In about one-third of states, if a family does not feed its children, it is only considered neglect if the parents knew about food assistance programs and deliberately chose not to use them. In cases where families simply need financial help to provide for children, investigators would put the family in touch with resources in the community, such as the WIC program.

If investigators suspect that children are in danger because of neglect and not just poverty, they can arrange to have the family visited in their home by a doctor, nurse, or social worker. They can also have doctors schedule frequent follow-up appointments for children or arrange for the family to have a consultation with a social worker.

NEGLECT THROUGH INACTION

"Children depend on their parents to protect them. A parent who stands by, passively acquiescing to abuse, is also an abuser. The violent look to bystanders for cues, and they count passivity or indifference as endorsement."
–Ginger and Richard Rhodes, authors

Ginger Rhodes and Richard Rhodes. *Trying to Get Some Dignity: Stories of Triumph Over Childhood Abuse*. New York, NY: William Morrow and Company Inc., 1996, p. 120.

Some families may have religious beliefs that prevent them from seeking medical care. One example is the Christian Science religion, whose members believe only God—not doctors—can heal people. Even when their children are very sick, Christian Scientists rarely seek medical help. When a child dies because of lack of medical care, some states have tried the parents for child abuse. In Wisconsin in 2013, the parents of 11-year-old Kara Neumann were convicted of reckless homicide for not providing medical care for their daughter. Kara's parents believed she had come down with the flu, but the coroner determined she had died from complications from untreated and undiagnosed diabetes. Her parents believed she would be healed through prayer. They also believed that if she died, she would be raised from the dead. The judge ruled that it is a parent's duty to provide care.

Investigators also see cases of physical abuse that may fall into a gray area. In some cases, parents who meant to discipline their children have used corporal punishment that became too extreme. Sometimes, investigators believe parents are trying their best and that the abuse was an isolated incident. They may feel that the child is not in any immediate danger. In cases such as this, investigators may arrange for the family to receive support from community resources. For example, they might arrange for parents to take parenting classes to help them learn ways to discipline children that do not involve corporal punishment. Alternatively, they might arrange for regular home visits from a nurse or social worker.

Building a Case

If investigators can substantiate that abuse or neglect definitely occurred, the next step is to preserve the evidence. This generally means taking the child to see a doctor or nurse for a physical exam. The evidence of child abuse and neglect is generally best documented by a doctor or nurse. In cases where neglect is suspected, doctors can evaluate whether a child is developing normally for their age. Blood tests can show whether a child is getting enough of certain nutrients, such as iron.

In cases where investigators suspect physical abuse, doctors can evaluate whether a child's physical injuries seem to be normal for the child's age and typical activities. For example, babies who have not learned to walk rarely bruise themselves. Older children who do run around and fall frequently are still unlikely to bruise themselves in well-protected parts of the body. For example, children do not often bruise their upper arms, upper legs, neck, or buttocks in an accidental fall. If children have been burned, doctors suspect that the burn happened deliberately if it is very symmetrical.

When doctors find injuries that are suspicious, doctors or investigators need to take photographs. These are important because later, lawyers representing the child can include them as exhibits in their legal documents. The photographs may be important if the state asks a judge to issue a restraining order preventing an abusive caregiver from having contact with a child.

Medical guidelines for documenting child abuse state that doctors should take color pictures of each injury from at least two angles and include a ruler or coin in the picture so the size of the injury is clear. Although it is important legally to have this proof of a child's injuries, the process of taking photographs can be very hard on children. Social worker Marc Parent remembered watching two detectives take photos of a child's bruises. He wrote,

> They stretched the reluctant Davey prostrate on a white table to photograph close-ups of his ripening bruises ...They'd have Davey freeze in the most impossible display of his injuries as they moved in close with the camera only to find the flash units hadn't charged. Davey would strain to hold his position as the men waited for what seemed like an eternity, through the whine of the recharging [cameras]. The child winced and whimpered as they began, but by the time they'd finished, he had closed his eyes and let them have their way, assuming the wayward positions they put him in like he'd done it a thousand times.[14]

Help within the Home

Child welfare investigators are required by law to avoid removing children from their families if they possibly can. Most states require investigators to make what are called "reasonable efforts" to keep families together. There are two reasons for this. First, states recognize that parents have a right to raise their own children without interference from the government unless something unusual, such as an extreme case of abuse or neglect, has occurred. Second, research shows that children are better off with their families unless they are in immediate danger. It used to be more common for investigators to remove children from families, especially if parents were addicted to drugs or alcohol. However, studies have shown that even babies who are born to mothers with a drug addiction fare better if they remain with their mothers while the mothers go through a substance abuse rehabilitation, or rehab, program. Additionally, the mothers are more likely to complete a rehab program when they have their babies with them.

To keep families together, investigators will make a safety plan and give the family the option to accept voluntary services—those that a family is not required by law or by a court order to participate in. They try to identify resources that will help the family with its unique set of stresses. For example, if parents have a substance abuse problem, investigators can arrange for them to go through a rehab program or attend Alcoholics Anonymous (AA) meetings. If adults need help with parenting skills, they can attend parenting classes. Investigators also often arrange for families to receive regular home visits from social workers or visiting nurses. They may arrange free child care for the family. They may also arrange for members of the family to receive health care for mental or physical illnesses. Visits from social workers often help motivate parents and caregivers to be more aware of how they treat their children.

In some cases, though, investigators feel they must remove children from their homes for the children's own safety. Even if an investigation does not substantiate a charge of child

Reasons for Removal to Foster Care (2015)

(type)	(number)	(percent)
neglect	161,791	61
drug abuse parent	85,937	32
caretaker inability to cope	37,243	14
physical abuse	34,647	13
child behavior problem	30,124	11
inadequate housing	27,002	10
parent incarceration	21,006	8
alcohol abuse parent	14,978	6
abandonment	12,363	5
sexual abuse	10,330	4
drug abuse child	6,085	2
child disability	4,514	2
relinquishment	2,569	1
parent death	2,019	1
alcohol abuse child	1,320	0

As this information from the U.S. Department of Health and Human Services shows, children are placed in foster care for a variety of reasons, with neglect and drug abuse by the parent being the top reasons.

abuse, children may be removed from their homes if conditions in the home are unsafe. Of families investigated for child abuse in 2015, 61 percent of children were removed because of neglect and 32 percent due to their parents' drug use. In the best of cases, children are placed with family members, such as grandparents, aunts, uncles, and adult siblings. This kind of foster care is called kinship care. If no family member is willing or able to take the children, however, they must be placed with a foster family they are not related to or in a group home.

April Smith was the 32-year-old mother of three children: a 16-month-old, a 4-year-old, and a 12-year-old. Investigators visiting her home found it littered with broken glass, animal and human feces, moldy food, and hazardous electrical fixtures. Smith and her boyfriend were addicted to drugs. They sometimes left home for days at a time, leaving the 12-year-old to babysit both of her younger siblings and a pair of unrelated 7-year-olds. When they were home, Smith's boyfriend abused her in front of the children. The 12-year-old had tried to commit suicide and was performing poorly in school. In this case, child welfare investigators removed the children from the home.

Sometimes, investigators must make difficult decisions, and frequently, there is no perfect answer. It seemed obvious to social workers that Smith's home was not a suitable environment for children. However, investigators also realized that removing the children and placing them in foster care was not ideal, either, because they were not able to place all three children in the same foster home. In this case, authorities had to make the best choice for the children even though neither choice was ideal.

There are also times when children are removed from their families even though authorities know the parent has not done anything wrong. In these cases, investigators believe that the parents, while not abusive, may not be able to protect children from the abuse of someone else in the family or neighborhood. Marc Parent recalled a case in which doctors at an emergency room determined that an eight-year-old girl was being raped regularly. She lived with her mother and younger siblings, and investigators were able to determine that her mother had done nothing wrong. Social workers spent hours trying to determine who the rapist was, keeping the family safe at the hospital in the meantime. However, they could not find out who was abusing the girl, and they believed that if they sent her home, the rape would continue. They did not believe the girl's mother would be able to protect her or any of her siblings from being abused again. Finally, they decided to take the children into temporary custody. Parent described what happened next:

> Security closed in on the family, and as they did, Lucia [the children's mother] screamed something in Spanish and the four of them bolted to the far wall, knocking through trays, stretchers, and equipment. Alex and I followed them quickly along with security and cornered them together where the children crouched down to the floor, rolling themselves into a tight ball around their mother … The ball grew tighter as we closed in; each of the kids wrapping their fists around whatever clothing on their mother they could find …
>
> It took every single guard to split it apart … Many of the nurses looked away. You know it's bad when the ER staff looks away. One by one the screaming children were [removed] from the rumbling pile, each one emerging with a burly-armed escort.[15]

Fortunately, when children are removed from their home, the removal is not necessarily permanent. The goal of almost every caseworker who removes a child from the family is someday to bring the child back to that family. The process of bringing the child back is called reunification. According to Judge Mary Triggiano of Milwaukee County Circuit Court in Wisconsin, the process of reunification should begin as soon as a child is removed from a home. Social workers should immediately begin arranging visits between a child's foster family and birth family. It is important for the process to begin quickly, because most reunifications take place in the first year after a child is placed in foster care. In 2015, 51 percent of children in foster care were reunited with their parents in under a year. Most children who are placed in foster care will eventually be reunited with their families. Before reunification happens, investigators work with the birth family to try to prevent any future acts of neglect or abuse.

Foster Parents Are Always Needed

Certain requirements for becoming a foster parent vary from state to state, but there are some requirements that are similar. Most states require that responsible individuals must be at least 21 years old to apply to be a foster parent. Foster parents do not have to be married and do not have to own their own homes. Some work outside the home and already have their own children, while others do not. Each state requires a physical exam to ensure that the potential caregivers are in good health. Additionally, they must have stable mental and emotional health. This is because working with children who have been neglected and abused can be emotionally exhausting for the caregiver.

People who want to become foster parents must first fill out an application with their local department of child and family services. They must go through a criminal background check to make sure that they have never been convicted of a crime or investigated for child abuse. The state agency will visit a prospective foster home to inspect it for safety and interview potential foster parents. Potential foster parents must also show that they can afford to meet the expenses of a family. The state reimburses foster families for some expenses, such as meals. However, foster families are responsible for paying their own rent and for occasional expenses such as clothes and school fees.

Foster families can provide a safe place for a child to heal.

Preventing Child Abuse

Child abuse can result from overstressed and overwhelmed caregivers. Parents and caregivers who abuse their children may require support and child care training in order to stop abusive behaviors. In many families, recurring child abuse can be preventable with support and treatment. Other families may lose custody of their children because child welfare investigators think of the well-being of the child above all else. Investigators carefully determine whether removing children from the home would be best and how to support the family.

Is Home the Best Place?

Twenty-three-year-old Rochanda Madry of Minneapolis, Minnesota, had five children and was overwhelmed. Most of the time, she raised her children by herself with no help. One day, she left her youngest daughter, who was still a baby, in the care of a friend. The friend lost control with the baby, and Madry took her daughter to the hospital with a swollen, chipped elbow joint. Because babies are unlikely to injure their own elbows, Madry's family was investigated. Even though she did not injure the baby herself, Madry was later charged with neglect. She lost custody of her children temporarily and was ordered to take an eight-week parenting class. After the class, she regained custody of her children.

Madry was not happy about being blamed for an injury that her baby received in someone else's care. She was angry when her children were removed from her care, but she was pleased with

Parenting classes can help make home a safe place for a child.

the results of the parenting class that she took. She said she used to threaten and yell at her children to get them to obey her. After taking the class, she used time-outs to give both herself and her children time to cool off, and getting extra help with child care made it possible for her to study for her General Educational Development (GED) test. The diploma would make it possible for her to get a better job and earn more money to support her family.

Child welfare experts say that Madry's case, in some ways, is typical. Parents respond much more positively to help from the community in the form of classes, child care assistance, and other resources than they do to having their children removed from their home. Research shows that when children can remain with their families, they are often safer than they are in foster care. If parents commit acts of abuse and neglect because they are overwhelmed and under too much stress, child advocates argue, it may make more sense to prevent abuse by removing parental stress and by educating parents. It costs less for the community to provide parenting classes and even financial assistance in the form of food stamps and housing subsidies (money from the state to help pay for housing) than it does to go through the process of removing a child from the home, going to court, and providing foster care. Additionally, it is easier on both the parents and the children to have the state take action to support them than it is for the state to pull the family apart.

Models of Investigation

For these reasons, many states now choose to offer a gentler approach to preventing child abuse than they have in the past. This gentle approach to stopping child abuse, though, coexists with the older, more adversarial model. In theory, removing children from the home is an option that should only be resorted to in extreme cases, such as when children are in danger. However, some critics argue that investigators are too quick to remove children and that they place children in foster homes that are less safe than the children's own homes.

Some child welfare agencies are turning to a different model for investigating child abuse. Instead of investigating every report of child abuse, they classify each report based on the amount of risk to children that is involved. If a report is classified as high risk, the investigation proceeds in the traditional way. The child, parents, and caregivers are interviewed, and social workers visit the home and review the child's history. However, if a case is classified as being of low-to-moderate risk, social workers approach it differently. Instead of formally investigating, they do an assessment. They do not make a formal determination that the report of abuse is substantiated or unsubstantiated. However, they do find out what stresses the family is experiencing and offer help. Cases that are assessed this way may never make it into the court system. If the assessment were to show that children were at high risk, however, the response could be upgraded to a formal investigation.

This two-tiered approach to investigating abuse is referred to by different names. Some states call it a differential response, while others call it a dual track or alternative response. The purpose of this model is to focus on keeping families together as much as possible, offering help instead of threatening to remove a child from the home. In jurisdictions where a differential response has been tried, social workers have found that parents cooperate more with child welfare agencies. An assessment does not carry the same stigma as a child abuse investigation, so parents do not feel as though their family is under attack. Another issue is that there are so many child abuse cases that the state cannot afford to investigate each one formally. Using a differential response makes it possible to prioritize the cases in which children are in the most danger.

A GOOD FAMILY

"I've been through verbal abuse, physical abuse, sexual abuse, all the abuse that you can think of ... I ended up in three different foster homes ... I had one good foster family, one that taught me about morals and values. It was a pretty good family; it taught me about life."
—Lou Della Casey, former foster child

Quoted in Children's Defense Fund, The State of America's Children, 2005, p. 114. www.childrensdefense.org/site/DocServer/Greenbook2005.pdf?docID=1741.

Abusive Households:
Domestic Violence and Child Abuse

Some of the most dangerous families for children are those in which domestic violence occurs regularly. Research shows that domestic violence and child abuse tend to go hand in hand. About half of all child abuse cases occur in homes in which women are being battered by their spouses or partners, and about half of men who assault their spouses or partners also attack their children. Even those people who do not directly attack their children frequently end up hurting them accidentally when the children try to protect the parent being abused.

For example, Carol Johnson's partner beat her every day for four years. He caused her to have three miscarriages. She finally carried a son, Mark, to term, because her partner was in jail during the pregnancy. When Mark's father returned home from jail, he began beating Carol again. He did not attack Mark, but Mark got hurt anyway because he tried to get between his mother and father during beatings. "I knew he was going to kill us," Carol said, "but I didn't know how to leave or where to go."[16] She finally fled to another state when Mark's father was sent to jail again.

Carol was lucky that she did not lose custody of her son. Women whose partners assault them often lose custody of their children because child welfare investigators argue that these mothers have failed to protect their children from their fathers.

In cases of fatal child abuse, some of these women are prosecuted for crimes of omission, or failure to protect their children from abusive partners. Around 29 states have laws of omission or enabling child abuse, and only a few of these states provide an exception for a battered partner who was afraid for their life. One example of someone who was prosecuted for enabling abuse was June Webb, whose six-year-old son was murdered by her husband Keith. June had reported her husband for domestic violence multiple times, but he had never been prosecuted. When her son was killed, June was prosecuted for not seeking medical help for him and was sentenced to 10 years in prison.

Because domestic violence and child abuse are so closely connected, domestic violence agencies and child welfare organizations are beginning to work together to try to prevent both kinds of abuse. Battered women's shelters are beginning to be recognized by states as safe places where women can take their children without fear of having their children taken from them. Child welfare investigators making a safety plan for a family may require abusive partners to go through counseling or take anger management classes. Additionally, domestic violence agencies and child welfare organizations are forming partnerships to educate the community about all the different kinds of violence that can affect families.

Creating Awareness in the Community

Organizations dedicated to the well-being of children often run campaigns to raise community awareness of child abuse and domestic violence. Domestic violence awareness campaigns are generally conducted in October, which is Domestic Violence Awareness Month. Child abuse awareness campaigns are run in April, which is Child Abuse Prevention Month. During these campaigns, agencies not only educate the public about the existence of family violence but also try to encourage families to find peaceful alternatives to violence in everyday situations.

While most organizations run their annual child abuse awareness campaigns in April, they provide year-round support to parents. Child abuse hotlines are also available year-round, as well as parenting classes that parents can take during a pregnancy or while their children are still young. These classes educate parents about the kinds of behaviors that are normal for young children so parents do not punish their children for age-appropriate behavior. For example, some parents do not realize until they take a parenting class that it does not make sense to spank a six-month-old for crying.

Parenting instructors also teach parents nonviolent methods for punishment, such as time-outs, so parents have an option they can turn to when they feel that punishment is appropriate. For some parents, this is new information. When she was 20 years old, Malisa Grady took a parenting class.

When parents use appropriate punishments to correct a child's misbehavior, family life in general is happier and less stressful for everyone.

It was offered by the Illinois Department of Children and Family Services. "Before I took the class, [I thought] I was a usual parent," Grady said. "If a child did something, I'd hit her ... Now I talk to my kids more."[17] Marquita Brand added: "I used to get frustrated a lot ... But [the instructors] taught me how to sit down and talk to the children, and how to give them time-out."[18]

Medical Partners

Experts say the most effective child abuse prevention programs are the ones that target mothers who are still pregnant or parents whose children are newborns. The most widespread of these programs is the Nurse-Family Partnership (NFP), which is used in 42 states across the country.

Home visits by nurses form the cornerstone of the NFP program. Nurses begin visiting mothers while they are still pregnant. They visit low-income, at-risk mothers who are pregnant with their first child. Because they come to a woman's home, the pregnant mother is less likely to miss her appointment than she would be if she had to go to a clinic. The nurses help mothers make good choices about prenatal care and can offer advice about nutrition and exercise. Nurses continue to visit families until the new baby reaches the age of two. They provide parenting education as well as offer counseling and advice to mothers about life choices involving family planning, education, and finding a job.

Out Is the Only Way Through

Child welfare investigators, however, must also find ways to help children who have already been abused. The laws of most states require that social workers make reasonable efforts to help families keep their children safe without removing the children from the family. This means that social workers must offer help. They may offer to enroll the parents in parenting classes, help

Parenting classes can help parents of all races, economic backgrounds, and sexes learn how to handle the challenges of raising a child.

parents apply for child care or housing subsidies, or help parents go through the process of registering for unemployment benefits or food stamps. They may also direct parents to specific programs such as substance abuse treatment centers or clinics that provide low-cost health care. Any or all of these kinds of programs could be included in a family safety plan that child welfare investigators would prepare for a family. The plan would include a timeline listing each goal and when it should be completed. For many families, these plans do help.

In many cases, though, investigators are convinced that children will remain in danger if they stay in their homes. In 2015, child protection workers removed approximately 25 percent of abused or neglected children from their homes and placed them in foster care—more than 400,000 children entered foster care at some point during the year. They entered family foster homes, group homes, or residential treatment centers. Not all of them stayed in foster care for long. The average foster care child is eight years old, lives with a relative or nonrelative foster family, and has been in foster care for less than two years.

The growing opioid drug crisis in the United States has led to a large number of children in foster care or being raised by family members who are not their parents. In 2016, 2,171 children were removed from their homes due to parental drug abuse, more than double the number of children removed from their homes in 2006.

In Georgia, 40 percent of children placed in foster care were removed from their homes due to their parents' use of drugs. Foster care workers across the United States have also seen an increase in young children and infants requiring foster home placement. Some states have even adopted new child abuse laws to include parental opioid use. Highly addictive drugs such as heroin, morphine, and some prescription pain medications are considered opioids.

The Courts and Victims of Abuse

If investigators think children are in danger, they are able to get an emergency order authorizing the removal of the children from the home right away. Then, the family is asked to appear at a hearing that occurs after the children have already been placed in foster care.

The initial hearing should include all caregivers or parents in the household and the child or children in question. If appearing in court is stressful for children, though, the judge can choose to meet with the children in chambers (the judge's office). According to the late Judge William G. Jones, "The initial hearing should establish a supportive atmosphere in which parents are treated with dignity and respect. It is a process that should focus on understanding the problems the case presents and solving them as quickly as possible so the family can be reunited safely."[19]

In the initial hearing, the court must make decisions about how to address the family's immediate needs. The initial hearing, however, is only the first of several. There may also be an adjudication, or fact-finding, hearing. Adjudication is the process of going to court and presenting evidence at a hearing before a judge. In an adjudication hearing, the court hears evidence and tries to determine what the facts are. Finally, there is a disposition hearing, in which the court decides what kind of help the child needs and whether it is necessary to order services to be provided to the family. In some cases, the court might decide to keep the family's children in foster care while the parents resolve their own problems. For example, a judge might feel that children should be cared for by someone other than the parents if the parents are about to go through rehabilitation for a drug or alcohol dependency. In other cases, the court may order that children be reunited with their parents immediately but also require the parents to go through counseling or rehabilitation.

Some juvenile courts across the country have begun to offer mediation services as an alternative to adjudication. Mediation is a gentler process for families. During mediation, families meet together with a court employee who helps the family think through their problems and work together to devise solutions. If the family can come up with a reasonable plan, the court may approve it. If not, the family may still be able to agree about some issues, shortening the amount of time necessary to go through adjudication.

When families get enough help and support early in the lives of their children, abusive situations may not arise at all. This is the ideal outcome, but many children do experience abuse and neglect. These children need help to make their homes safe places in which to grow up. They may also need help recovering from their experiences. With treatment for their physical and emotional injuries, children can begin to feel safe and secure again. Many adults who were abused as

Too Old for Foster Care?

There are several ways children can leave foster care. They can be reunited with their original families, placed with relatives, or adopted by a new family. Many children, however, leave foster care by aging out of it. This means that they reach the age of 18 while still living with a foster family. When children in foster care reach the age of 18, the state no longer acts as their guardian. They are expected to leave foster care and take care of themselves. In 2015, more than 20,000 children aged out of foster care.

Misty Stenslie Claassen, former director of the Foster Care Alumni of America, spent 12 years in foster care as a child and aged out of the program. She said of her experience, "A social worker here, a judge there, hundreds of different people over the years, and yet somehow even with all those people looking out for me and taking care of me, I aged out with no family at all. On Tuesday you're a kid and somebody's there to take care of you, and on Wednesday you're an adult; and nobody's there."[1]

Children who age out of foster care often are not prepared to care for themselves. Almost half of children who age out of foster care leave without having earned their high school diploma or General Educational Development (GED). Without a high school diploma or its equivalent, it is hard to get a job and earn a living. About one-third of these young people end up living below the poverty level and working in jobs that do not provide health insurance. Additionally, they are three to seven times more likely to have chronic health issues and mental illnesses. One-quarter have post-traumatic stress disorder (PTSD) from the abuse they have endured. Nearly 40 percent of children who age out of foster care become homeless; 20 percent of them are homeless the instant they turn 18.

1. Quoted in Chelsea-Badeau, "No Kid Should Age Out of Foster Care Alone in America," Foster Club, May 28, 2009. www.fosterclub.com/_advocacy/news/no-kid-should-age-out-foster-care-alone-america.

children enter professions in which they help other children regain their feelings of trust and security.

OUT OF THE SHADOWS: TALKING ABOUT ABUSE

"It happens every day. It happens in the best of families. It happens in the best of communities, so it's time. We've got to open our eyes to it and we've gotta start talking about it." —Monique Gorman, community advocate at the Gulf Coast Children's Advocacy Center

Quoted in Leanna Scachetti, "Panhandle Experts Report More Cases of Child Abuse Every Year," WTVY, April 28, 2017. www.wtvy.com/content/news/420742773.html.

Healing Old Wounds

"Trauma, by definition, is the result of exposure to an inescapably stressful event that overwhelms a person's coping mechanisms,"[20] wrote psychiatrist Bessel van der Kolk. Therapists and other professionals who work with abuse survivors understand the trauma caused by abuse. Many survivors develop PTSD, which can cause extreme distress for decades after the abuse has ended—children who grow up in abusive environments face a lifetime of complications. In 2000, The National Child Traumatic Stress Network was created by the United States Congress as part of the Children's Health Act. The network connects child abuse survivors with doctors and therapists across the United States. By 2009, the Network had found that only a quarter of the children treated met the criteria for PTSD. Instead, child abuse survivors were being diagnosed with bipolar disorder, attention deficit hyperactivity disorder (ADHD), conduct disorders, reactive attachment disorder, and separation anxiety. Many children had more than one diagnosis.

In order to better treat the complex issues of child abuse survivors, the Network proposed a new diagnosis that they hoped would be included in the *Diagnostic and Statistical Manual of Mental Disorders, Fifth Edition (DSM-5)*. Developmental Trauma Disorder (DTD) would be diagnosed in children who were exposed to prolonged trauma from caregivers and present symptoms related to but unique from PTSD. Although DTD was not accepted as a formal diagnosis in the *DSM-5*, a subtype of PTSD was added that was specific to children six years old and younger.

Long-Term Effects of Abuse

Physical abuse and neglect cause physical injuries and health problems such as malnutrition and anemia. However, recovering from physical injuries and malnutrition is just the beginning of the healing process for most child abuse survivors. Even after a child recovers physically from abuse, emotional injuries remain. Children with PTSD may suffer from unwanted memories of their abuse. Some have flashbacks during the day and nightmares at night. Others develop anxiety or depression. They may be startled easily. They may find it difficult to trust other people or to be affectionate. Some are very irritable and may be aggressive or violent themselves. Many use drugs or alcohol to try to escape from their emotions and end up with a substance abuse problem as well.

Child abuse can have a lifetime effect on physical and mental health.

Abuse survivors who do not develop PTSD may suffer from other psychological disorders. They may suffer from low self-esteem or become suicidal. Children who have been abused are more likely to develop psychological disorders such as schizophrenia. They are also more likely to develop behavior problems. They may tend to argue with adults and defy authority. Many have trouble paying attention in school or following instructions. Boys, especially, tend to develop behavior problems such as fighting or destroying property. These behaviors may continue into adulthood.

Abuse Can Alter the Brain

Psychiatrists are beginning to find, too, that the stress of abuse can affect a very young child's developing brain. Some babies who have been abused grow up unable to accept comfort from others. Preschool children who have been abused tend to have developmental delays. Developmental delays can mean, for example, that a child learns to speak later than other children or does not speak clearly. A delay can also cause a child to take longer to learn to do physical activities that other children do easily, such as standing on one foot or holding a pencil. However, there are also many medical reasons why a child might be developmentally delayed—developmental delays are not, by themselves, a sign of abuse or neglect.

Psychologists have also found that preschoolers who have been abused have a harder time making full use of play materials at their preschools. They tend to touch or pound toys instead of playing with them. Some severely neglected children have never learned how to play. Instead of pretending to iron with a toy iron, for example, a preschooler who has been abused or neglected might pound the iron repetitively on the floor or put the iron in their mouth. Other children reenact their experiences of abuse in their pretend play.

The social skills of abused preschoolers also lag behind. These children tend to move quickly from one activity to another, finding it difficult to focus on one thing. They do not feel self-confident initiating a conversation with other children. They may seem hypervigilant, which means they constantly monitor what is happening around them to make sure the situation is safe. Children who have been physically abused or neglected sometimes act out in aggressive, disruptive ways in the classroom. They may hit or bite other children or destroy property. Children who have been sexually abused, on the other hand, more often become passive, withdrawn, and quiet.

HEALING PRACTICES

"So often survivors have had their experiences denied, trivialized, or distorted. Writing is an important avenue for healing because it gives you the opportunity to define your own reality. You can say: This did happen to me. It was that bad. It was the fault & responsibility of the adult. I was—and am—innocent."
—Ellen Bass, author of *The Courage to Heal: A Guide for Women Survivors of Child Sexual Abuse*

Quoted in "Quotes About Childhood Abuse," Goodreads, accessed September 18, 2017. www.goodreads.com/quotes/tag/childhood-abuse.

The Body Remembers

Child abuse survivors often develop symptoms in their bodies that cannot be explained by a medical exam. Children may have headaches, stomachaches, or feel unusually tired all the time. Some develop diarrhea, constipation, or urinary tract infections that have no physical explanation. These symptoms are generally classified as a somatic disorder, which means that they have a psychological, not a physical, cause. A few therapists prefer to call these symptoms "body memories," because they feel that the symptoms are connected with the body's memory of having been abused. The late therapist and researcher Alice Miller wrote,

> The truth about our childhood is stored up in our body, and although we can repress it, we can never alter it. Our intellect can be deceived, our feelings manipulated, our perceptions confused, and our body tricked with medication. But someday the body will present its bill, for it is as incorruptible as a child who, still whole in spirit, will accept no compromises or excuses, and it will not stop tormenting us until we stop evading the truth.[21]

Past trauma can reappear as physical pain.

In 1990, a team of researchers conducted the Adverse Childhood Experiences (ACE) study to discover the effects of child abuse. They developed a point system for each abusive event reported, including physical abuse, witnessing domestic abuse, and the divorce of parents. The ACE study found that 87 percent of patients had 2 or more adverse events. Those who scored four or more points—one in every six respondents—were more likely to abuse drugs and alcohol, have poor school performance, and suffer from chronic or long-lasting conditions such as obesity, heart disease, and cancer. The study calculated that child abuse was the most costly epidemic in the United States. Additional studies have confirmed the ACE findings. Childhood trauma stays in the body and can affect someone for life.

Triggering Memories

Abuse survivors who have behavioral problems tend not to have them at random times. Frequently, something happens to trigger a memory of their abuse. This is called the trauma cycle. It is similar to a flashback. In a flashback, the survivor re-experiences the abuse, seeing the same sights, hearing the same sounds, or feeling the same physical sensations that happened during the abusive experience. However, in the trauma cycle, survivors may simply re-experience a part of the abuse, such as the feelings and emotions that went with it. These feelings rise up in a survivor because something happens to trigger them. The trigger could be anything that reminds the survivor of the abuse—an event or even the words or tone of voice used by a teacher or a friend.

When a trigger event occurs, survivors lose their ability to think rationally. They have a fight-or-flight reaction in which their bodies are pumped full of adrenaline. The survivor's limbic system—the part of the brain responsible for basic functions such as the need for food and sleep—takes over. Bruce Perry, a doctor who specializes in pediatric brain development, explained that trigger events make children feel threatened. In response to a threat, the heart rate increases, breathing quickens, and different parts of the brain take over. Perry said,

> The more threatened we become, the more "primitive" (or regressed) our style of thinking and behaving becomes. When a traumatized child is in a state of alarm (because they are thinking about the trauma, for example) they will be less capable of concentrating, they will be more anxious and they will pay more attention to "non-verbal" cues such as tone of voice, body posture and facial expressions.[22]

When this happens, survivors become hyperalert and need help to become calm again. Therapists respond when this happens by using a soft, level voice and by using neutral body language.

For many survivors, authority figures can trigger the trauma cycle to recur. In their birth families, these survivors may have been subjected to parents or caregivers who insisted on obedience and who also abused them. These survivors feel more secure if they are in an environment where they have more choices about what they do and do not want to do next. When they are subjected to authority, such as the authority of a classroom teacher, these children may appear to have behavior problems. Girls may seem not to be paying attention. Boys may seem hyperactive. Both may have difficulty doing math problems, for example, when they are called to the front of the classroom. It is hard to do schoolwork after something has triggered a memory of abuse, because the memory brings up a variety of strong emotions. Therapists respond to this kind of situation by trying to give children more control. Perry explained, "If a child is given some choice or some element of control in an activity or in an interaction with an adult, they will feel more safe, comfortable and will be able to feel, think and act in a more 'mature' fashion."[23]

Reliving Experiences

Survivors of child abuse often experience flashbacks, even years after the abuse is over. A flashback is a memory that is so intense that it feels as though the survivor is reliving the experience. Some flashbacks are so real that the person experiencing them sees, hears, and feels the abuse happening all over again. Other flashbacks are more fragmentary—a survivor might remember just an image or a feeling that dates back to the abuse. Either way, flashbacks can be very stressful and even terrifying.

Survivors who experience flashbacks often find that counseling and psychotherapy can be very helpful. During a flashback, it can help to open one's eyes and look around, making sure to notice things that make one feel safe. Some survivors carry a special rock or other object in a pocket and hold the object during a flashback as a way of trying to feel more secure. It can also help to notice what triggers a flashback—what words, images, smells, or sounds cause those memories to return.

Healing Is Possible

Healing from child abuse does not happen quickly. Survivors of child abuse develop many coping mechanisms in order to survive. As they grow older, these skills may turn against them. For instance, in an abusive household, a child may learn never to speak up or stand up for themselves. Once the child is an adult, they may find it hard to ask for what they need. This can impact work, school, and intimate relationships. Survivors may judge themselves for not being able to cope in the world like everyone else.

Survivors may blame themselves for the abuse or act out in ways that cause them to feel shame. These shameful feelings can cause a survivor to be critical of themselves. They may speak poorly about themselves and let others do the same. Survivors often think they deserve the negative things that happen to them. Researchers have begun to look at self-compassion as a way to heal PTSD and other trauma from child abuse.

With self-compassion, survivors can learn to love themselves. Instead of taking the blame for abuse, self-compassion helps survivors feel connected to their pain. They begin to feel empathy for themselves instead of anger or shame. One of the leading researchers in self-compassion, Kristin Neff, said, "Instead of seeing ourselves as a problem to be fixed … self-kindness allows us to see ourselves as valuable human beings who are worthy of care."[24] Self-compassionate ways of understanding allow survivors to release the shame and anger they may carry. Survivors can learn that they deserve good things, and when bad things do happen, they should not always blame themselves.

EMPATHY AND FORGIVENESS FOR THE ABUSER

"Although she's living and I still get close to confronting her and asking her questions about this stuff, I back off and say, Well, I'm sure she was a victim too. She couldn't have been that way if she hadn't suffered some sort of abuse in childhood. You want to forgive. That's the thing. You want to be done with it. You don't want to keep stirring it up. You feel that it was all your fault in the first place."
–David Ray, childhood abuse survivor

Quoted in Ginger Rhodes and Richard Rhodes, *Trying to Get Some Dignity: Stories of Triumph Over Childhood Abuse*. New York, NY: William Morrow and Company Inc., 1996, p. 126.

Sometimes forgiveness is possible.

Reaching Out to Kids

One high school teacher who worked with emotionally disturbed children explained why feeling safe is so important: "The first thing you have to provide for them is a safe, comfortable environment," he said. "Number one, they need to develop a feeling of trust and comfort and security. And it needs to go for a long period of time—it's got to be something that they can count on day in and day out."[25]

Former foster child Robert Kendall agreed. He said,

> Deep down, kids all want the same stuff. They all want to be loved, they all want a family. And they all want to know why they didn't have a family and they weren't loved. They're trying to figure out why everything happened to them and can it ever be okay ... so that they can say to themselves, "It will be okay, and I can relax, and these people aren't going to hurt me."[26]

Psychotherapy can help children and families heal.

Children cannot really begin the process of healing until they feel safe and secure. Psychotherapy is sometimes called talk therapy or counseling. It means taking time to talk about the abuse and its continuing effects. Psychotherapists try to help children understand that what happened to them was not their fault and to find ways to process and release their memories of abuse. Therapists working with young children often use art therapy and play therapy as well. Art therapy means using creative processes, such as music, dance, movement, drama, drawing, painting, and poetry, to work through negative memories and emotions. Play therapy is a type of therapy aimed at very young children who may have trouble expressing their feelings in words. They can use dolls and toys to help them tell a therapist about what happened to them and how they feel about it.

As they talk with children about abuse, therapists try to focus on the positive—the fact that children survived and are still here to tell the tale of what happened. Bessel van der Kolk said, "One of the first things you need to ask is, how did you survive this? … This is amazing that you're still here. It's amazing that you still have the guts to go on with your life. What is allowing you to function? What are you good at? What gives you comfort?"[27]

In his TED Talk called "A Child of the State," British poet Lemn Sissay read off a list of famous characters in books who had been fostered, adopted, or orphaned. These characters include some of society's most loved heroes, such as Harry Potter, Luke Skywalker, Batman, and Superman. The experiences of these heroes have helped children who were abused and placed in foster care and given them comfort. Writer Nikki Grey reflected on how one of these heroes, Harry Potter, helped her through her time in foster care:

The Harry Potter books brought me comfort in the darkest period of my life. They helped me escape reality and allowed me precious opportunities to experience wonder. The story of an orphan who beat the odds against him gave me hope that maybe I could do the same thing. Although making it through foster care without losing hope was no easy feat, I was not even close to as brave as Harry

Potter. But when J.K. Rowling wrote about a little boy who went from living underneath a staircase to becoming the most significant wizard of his time, she gave me someone to believe in.[28]

Sissay said, "Children in care, who've had a life in care, deserve the right to own and live the memory of their own childhood."[29] Children who have lived through often horrible things have a right to understand their story, to heal, and to move on to a better life. Healing often comes through talking to other people and understanding their own stories.

Talking to a Professional

Many survivors of abuse find that talk therapy helps them reduce or manage the symptoms of depression, anxiety, flashbacks, and attention disorders. There are many kinds of talk therapy, including psychotherapy, cognitive behavioral therapy, and others. To receive psychotherapy, survivors must go to a licensed psychologist—a doctor who has a Ph.D. and has been licensed by the state to treat mental disorders. Other types of therapists may have a master's degree in social work. It is important to find a therapist who can work with survivors on the healing they need. Not all survivors feel they need talk therapy. However, those who sometimes think of committing suicide or who consider hurting themselves or others can benefit from seeing a psychologist or psychiatrist.

Talk therapy is also helpful for survivors who have trouble functioning in everyday life because of their symptoms. For example, some survivors have trouble concentrating in school or at work because of their feelings of anxiety. Others have flashbacks that interfere with their ability to function normally during the day.

Some survivors may feel that medication can help them cope with depression and suicidal thoughts. A psychiatrist can prescribe medication and work with survivors and their therapists to provide well-rounded care.

Physical and Mental Healing Tools

Meditation can help many survivors. Some types of meditation include mindfulness-based stress reduction, or MBSR. MBSR teaches a non-judgmental understanding of the body. Through MBSR, survivors can learn to quiet their thoughts. They may be able to approach bad memories without shame or fear. In combination with therapy, MBSR can aid in the healing process.

Healing can also take place in moving meditation through the practice of martial arts or yoga. In fact, any physical practice that a survivor enjoys, whether it be taking karate or yoga classes or trying out for a sport at school, can help in the healing process. Enjoyable physical activities give survivors good body memories to balance the negative memories of their traumatic experiences. The good memories, unfortunately, do not overwrite the bad ones. However, they provide a safe memory that survivors can try to go back to when they find themselves caught up in a flashback. They also provide a way for survivors to understand their bodies and feel strong and able.

Seeking Healing with Support

Alice Miller believed that anyone healing from abuse needed to find a healing witness. This witness would be able to show love and understanding to an abuse victim. "They will not need to avenge themselves violently for their wounds, or to poison their systems with drugs, if they have the luck to talk to others about their early experiences, and succeed in grasping the naked truth of their own tragedy,"[30] she wrote. A healing witness can help survivors develop compassion for themselves and their story.

Activities such as meditation or yoga can help with the healing process.

Home should be a safe and supportive place.

For all abuse survivors, the key to recovery is to take their own feelings seriously and understand how abuse has changed their lives. Survivors can work to develop a healthy sense of self-esteem, self-confidence, and a safe space to call home. Working with professional help and a loving community can help survivors walk the road to healing and recovery.

NOTES

Introduction: Home Can Be a Dangerous Place

1. Richard Pelzer, *A Brother's Journey: Surviving a Childhood of Abuse*. New York, NY: Warner, 2005, p. 1.

Chapter 1: Child Abuse in the United States

2. Gavin de Becker, *Protecting the Gift: Keeping Children and Teenagers Safe (and Parents Sane)*. New York, NY: Dial, 1999, p. 22.

3. Marc Parent, *Turning Stones: My Days and Nights with Children at Risk*. New York, NY: Harcourt Brace, 1996, p. 304.

4. Parent, *Turning Stones*, pp. 175–176.

5. Quoted in Ginger Rhodes and Richard Rhodes, *Trying to Get Some Dignity: Stories of Triumph Over Childhood Abuse*. New York, NY: William Morrow and Company Inc., 1996, p. 69.

6. Quoted in Karen Gardner, "April Is Child Abuse Prevention Month: Patient Parents Get Rewards in This Promotion," *Frederick News-Post*, April 9, 1993, p. B-5.

7. J. Robert Shull, "Emotional and Psychological Child Abuse: Notes on Discourse, History, and Change," *Stanford Law Review*, July 1, 1999, p. 1665.

8. James Garbarino, Edna Guttman, and Janis Wilson Seeley, *The Psychologically Battered Child: Strategies for Identification, Assessment and Intervention*. San Francisco, CA: Jossey-Bass, 1986, p. 12.

Chapter 2: Abuse at Any Age

9. Quoted in Chris Berdik, "Poor Little Rich Kids," *Boston Magazine*, December 2003. www.bostonmagazine.com/2006/05/poor-little-rich-kids/.

10. Quoted in Dan Benson, "West Bend Man Charged with Abuse: 2-Month-Old Girl Put on Life Support," *Milwaukee Journal Sentinel*, August 14, 2008, p. B1.

11. Quoted in Benson, "West Bend Man Charged with Abuse," p. B1.

Chapter 3: Investigating Child Abuse

12. Quoted in "Trauma and Dissociation in Children," Cavalcade Productions, accessed September 12, 2017. www.cavalcadeproductions.com/traumaanddissociation.html.

13. Dave Pelzer, *A Child Called "It": One Child's Courage to Survive*. Deerfield Beach, FL: Health Communications, 1995, pp. 9–10.

14. Parent, *Turning Stones*, pp. 83–84.

15. Parent, *Turning Stones*, pp. 284–285.

Chapter 4: Preventing Child Abuse

16. Quoted in Stephanie Walton, "When Violence Hits Home: Responding to Domestic Violence in Families with Kids Requires a Coordinated Effort to Help the Victim and Protect the Children," *State Legislatures*, June 2003, p. 31.

17. Quoted in Lisa Jones, "Why Are We Beating Our Children? An Upsurge in Child Abuse Cases Raises New Questions," *Ebony*, March 1993, p. 81.

18. Quoted in Jones, "Why Are We Beating Our Children?," p. 82.

19. William G. Jones, *Working with the Courts in Child Protection*, U.S. Department of Health and Human Services, 2006, p. 28. www.childwelfare.gov/pubs/usermanuals/courts/courts.pdf.

Chapter 5: Healing Old Wounds

20. Bessel van der Kolk, MD, "Posttraumatic Stress Disorder and Memory," *Psychiatric Times*, March 1, 1997. www.psychiatrictimes.com/printpdf/157698.

21. Alice Miller, *Thou Shalt Not Be Aware: Society's Betrayal of the Child*. New York, NY: Farrar Straus Giroux, 1984, p. 319.

22. Bruce Perry MD, "Principles of Working with Traumatized Children," Scholastic, accessed September 13, 2017. www.scholastic.com/teachers/articles/teaching-content/principles-working-traumatized-children/.

23. Perry, "Principles of Working with Traumatized Children."

24. Quoted in Beverly Engel, "Healing the Shame of Childhood Abuse Through Self-Compassion," *Psychology Today*, January 15, 2015. www.psychologytoday.com/blog/the-compassion-chronicles/201501/healing-the-shame-childhood-abuse-through-self-compassion.

25. Quoted in "The Traumatized Child," Cavalcade Productions, accessed September 13, 2017. www.cavalcadeproductions.com/traumatized-children.html.

26. Quoted in "The Traumatized Child," Cavalcade Productions.

27. Quoted in "Severe Early Trauma," Cavalcade Productions, accessed September 13, 2017. www.cavalcadeproductions.com/childhood-trauma.html.

28. Nikki Grey, "How Harry Potter Helped Me Get Through Childhood as an Orphan," Hello Giggles, February 4, 2016. hellogiggles.com/news/how-harry-potter-helped-childhood-orphan/.

29. Lemn Sissay, "A Child of the State," TED video, 15:17, filmed June 2012. www.ted.com/talks/lemn_sissay_a_child_of_the_state/transcript.

30. Alice Miller, "The Essential Role of an Enlightened Witness in Society," Alice Miller, 1997. www.alice-miller.com/en/the-essential-role-of-an-enlightened-witness-in-society/.

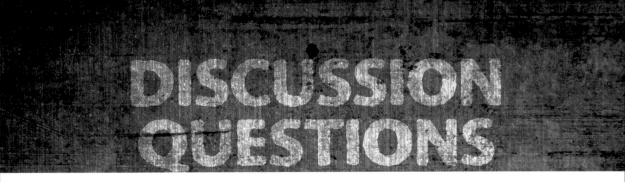

DISCUSSION QUESTIONS

Chapter 1:
Child Abuse in the United States

1. Who is a mandated reporter?
2. What is neglect?
3. Is emotional abuse as bad as physical abuse?

Chapter 2:
Abuse at Any Age

1. What are the most common characteristics of abuse perpetrators?
2. How are family poverty and child abuse related?
3. What age group has the highest risk of dying from abuse?

Chapter 3:
Investigating Child Abuse

1. What are voluntary services?
2. Why might a child not talk about abuse to investigators?
3. What is reunification?

Chapter 4:
Preventing Child Abuse

1. How does domestic violence affect the whole family?
2. List some reasonable efforts to help families stay together.
3. What happens when kids age out of foster care?

Chapter 5:
Healing Old Wounds

1. Explain how flashbacks and PTSD are related to child abuse.

2. How do meditation, yoga, and other physical activities help survivors?

3. How do compassion and a healing witness help survivors?

Childhelp

4350 E. Camelback Rd., Bldg. F250
Phoenix, AZ 85018
(480) 922-8212 (Hotline: (800) 422-4453)
www.childhelp.org

> Childhelp runs residential treatment programs and group homes for abused children and offers advocacy services for children. It also produces educational materials to increase public awareness about child abuse. Childhelp's child abuse hotline is staffed seven days a week, twenty-four hours a day.

Children's Defense Fund (CDF)

25 E. St. NW
Washington, D.C. 20001
(800) 233-1200
www.childrensdefense.org

> The Children's Defense Fund lobbies state legislatures and Congress about laws that affect children. It also works to educate the public and increase awareness about issues that disproportionately affect children, such as abuse and poverty. Child abuse is only one of several areas that the CDF focuses on.

Child Welfare League of America (CWLA)

727 15th St. NW, 12th Fl.
Washington, D.C. 20005
(202) 688-4200
www.cwla.org

> CWLA trains and educates child welfare workers and tries to increase awareness about child abuse among the public. It produces publications related to child abuse and offers conferences and classes.

National Council on Child Abuse and Family Violence (NCCAFV)
1025 Connecticut Ave. NW, Ste. 1000
Washington, D.C. 20036
(202) 429-6695
www.nccafv.org

> NCCAFV's mission is to connect community members, professionals, and volunteers to prevent domestic violence and child abuse. It staffs a hotline providing referrals to organizations that can help survivors to find a safe place to stay and to get legal help.

Rape, Abuse & Incest National Network (RAINN)
1220 L St NW
Washington, D.C. 20005
(800) 656-4673
www.rainn.org

> RAINN provides services to people affected by rape, abuse, incest, and additional traumas. Its website details the steps a witness to abuse can take to help a child report it to authorities. RAINN partners with more than 1,000 sexual assault services across the country.

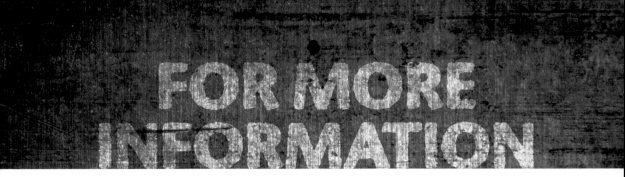

Books

Beam, Cris. *To the End of June: The Intimate Life of American Foster Care.* New York, NY: Mariner Books, 2014.
> Written by a foster mother, this book examines the foster care system, the children within the system, and what happens when they age out of it.

Krebs, Betsy, and Paul Pitcoff. *Beyond the Foster Care System: The Future for Teens.* Piscataway, NJ: Rutgers University Press, 2006.
> Krebs and Pitcoff examine the foster care system and discuss their argument that it does not serve teens well.

Olive, M. Foster. *Child Abuse and Stress Disorders.* New York, NY: Chelsea House, 2006.
> This book examines how child abuse contributes to stress disorders such as anxiety, depression, and PTSD.

Raja, Sheela, and Jaya Ashrafi. *The PTSD Survival Guide for Teens.* Oakland, CA: Instant Help Books, 2018.
> This book has strategies for those who have been diagnosed with PTSD or are dealing with a traumatic event. Included are skills based in a number of different therapies, information on diagnosis, and resources for recovery.

Van der Kolk, Bessel. *The Body Keeps Score: Brain, Mind, and Body in the Healing of Trauma.* New York, NY: Penguin Books, 2014.
> Psychiatrist Bessel van der Kolk describes decades of research into childhood trauma and PTSD. He gives simple explanations for complicated brain science and offers therapeutic paths to recovery.

Websites

"Alone Without a Home: A State-by-State Review of Laws Affecting Unaccompanied Youth"

www.nlchp.org/Alone_Without_A_Home

> This report by the National Law Center on Homelessness and Poverty details a state-by-state review of laws in the United States for serving these populations.

Child Welfare Information Gateway, U.S. Department of Health and Human Services

www.childwelfare.gov

> This website provides federal statistics and information on child abuse and neglect in the United States. It includes many fact sheets as well as links to state child welfare information agencies.

Darkness to Light

www.d2l.org

> This South Carolina–based organization provides information on preventing child abuse.

National Domestic Violence Hotline

www.thehotline.org

> The website of the National Domestic Violence Hotline includes articles about the connection between domestic violence and child abuse as well as statistics concerning the prevalence of domestic violence in the United States.

National Runaway Safeline

www.1800runaway.org

> This website includes statistics and information about runaway children as well as links to resources for children who are in a crisis.

INDEX

A

abusive head trauma, 37
adjudication, 69
Adverse Childhood Experiences (ACE), 77
aggression, 16, 73, 75
alcohol, 8, 17–18, 20, 26–28, 35, 52, 69, 73, 77
Alcoholics Anonymous (AA), 52
American Psychological Association, 16
anemia, 73
anxiety, 16, 24, 73, 85
art therapy, 84
attention deficit hyperactivity disorder (ADHD), 72

B

Bass, Ellen, 75
Batman, 84
de Becker, Gavin, 11
behavior problems, 37, 53, 74, 78
belittling, 8, 17, 24–25
Below, Michael, 33
bipolar disorder, 72
body memories, 75, 86
brain damage, 8, 37
Brand, Marquita, 66
Brookings Institute, 16

C

Carnes, Connie, 45
Casey, Lou Della, 61
cerebral palsy, 37
child abuse
    cases against pregnant women, 1973 to 2005, 18
    cases of suspected child abuse or neglect reported, 2015, 12
    children who died as a result of injuries, 2015, 36
    percent of children removed because of neglect, 2015, 54
    percent of children reunited with parents, 2015, 55
    screened-in cases, 2015, 12
    Straus and Gelles study and, 14
Child Abuse Prevention and Treatment Act (CAPTA), 16
Child Abuse Prevention Month, 63
Childhelp National Child Abuse Hotline, 42
child protection workers,

19–20, 29, 44, 68
Child Protective Services, 17, 23
Children's Health Act, 72
child welfare agencies, 12, 14, 23, 42, 44, 60–61
Christian Scientists, 16, 50
chronic health issues, 70
Claassen, Misty Stenslie, 70
Clark, Cari, 47
coma, 36
conduct disorders, 72
corporal punishment, 15–16, 45, 50
counseling, 63, 66, 69, 79, 84

D
Dale, Maren K., 32
death, 8, 10, 13, 30, 36, 38, 53
dehydrated, 30–31
depression, 16, 24, 27, 29, 32, 73, 85
developmental delays, 20, 74
Developmental Trauma Disorder (DTD), 72
Diagnostic and Statistical Manual of Mental Disorders, Fifth Edition (DSM-5), 72
disposition hearing, 69
domestic violence, 14, 24, 32, 62–63
Domestic Violence Awareness Month, 63
drugs, 8, 17–20, 26–28, 35, 44, 52–54, 68–69, 73, 77, 86

due process, 47

E
emotional abuse, 8, 13, 16, 23–25, 36
Every Child Matters, 13

F
false reporting, 12, 47
family violence, 63
fatal abuse, 36, 38
fight-or-flight, 78
flashback, 73, 77, 79, 85–86
food stamps, 60, 67
foster care, 10, 35, 48, 53–56, 60, 68–70, 84
Foster Care Alumni of America, 70
foster parents, 10, 56

G
Garbarino, James, 25
Gelles, Richard, 14–15, 17
General Education Development (GED), 60
Gorman, Monique, 71
Grady, Malisa, 63, 66
Gray, William, 48
Grey, Nikki, 84
group homes, 54, 68
Guttman, Edna, 25

H
Hamilton, Barbara, 20
Hazell, Ezra, 40, 42, 46
Hazell, Kristie, 40, 42
healing witness, 86

health insurance, 70
heroin, 18, 26, 68
homeless, 35, 70
homicide, 36–37, 50
housing subsidies, 60, 67
hyperalert, 78

I
initial hearing, 68–69
interviews, 45–46, 48, 61
intimidation, 25
investigation, 10, 23, 44, 47, 52, 60–61

J
Johnson, Carol, 62
Jones, Gregory, 30, 32–33
Jones, William G., 68

K
Kendall, Robert, 82

L
Leiby, Patricia, 24
Long, Rebecca, 30, 32
Lovell, Jessica Lee, 30, 32, 34

M
Madry, Rochanda, 58, 60
malnourished, 20, 30–31, 36, 44
malnutrition, 30, 73
mandated reporter, 12, 42–43
Marin, Katlyn, 29
mediation, 69
medication, 26, 29, 68, 75, 85
meditation, 86–87

mental illness, 19–20, 28–29, 70
Metz, Carrie, 26
Miller, Alice
    on repression, 75
    on talking about early experiences, 86
mindfulness-based stress reduction (MBSR), 86
morphine, 68
Muncy, Patricia, 24

N
name-calling, 25
National Center for Children in Poverty, 32
National Center on Shaken Baby Syndrome, 37
National Child Abuse and Neglect Data System, 36
National Child Traumatic Stress Network, 72
Neff, Kristin, 80
Neumann, Kara, 50
nightmares, 73
Nurse-Family Partnership (NFP), 66

O
opioids, 68

P
parenting classes, 8, 50, 52, 59–60, 63, 66
Pelzer, Dave, 45
Pelzer, Richard, 9–10, 45
perpetrator, 26–28, 30, 36–37

102 CHILD ABUSE: TRAGEDY AND TRAUMA

Perry, Bruce, 78–79
Petit, Michael, 13
photographs, 51
Pomeroy, Jon, 30, 32
post-traumatic stress disorder (PTSD), 70, 72–74, 80
Potter, Harry, 84–85
poverty, 27, 32–33, 49, 70
pregnancy, 62–63
psychiatrists, 72, 74, 85
psychologists, 17, 25, 74, 85
psychotherapy, 79, 83–85

R

Ray, David, 80
Ray, Kenisha Q., 23
reactive attachment disorder, 72
rehabilitation program, 44
residential treatment centers, 68
restraining order, 51
reunification, 20, 55–56, 69–70
Rhodes, Ginger and Richard, 49
runaway children, 35

S

safety plan, 52, 63, 67
schizophrenia, 29, 74
Seeley, Janis Wilson, 25
self-compassion, 80
self-esteem, 74, 89
separation anxiety, 72
shaken baby syndrome, 21, 23, 37
Shull, J. Robert, 24

Sissay, Lemn, 84–85
Skywalker, Luke, 84
Smith, April, 54
somatic disorder, 75
Speller, Elsa, 24
Straus, Murray, 14–15, 17
substance abuse, 32, 44, 52, 67, 73
substantiated cases, 46
Superman, 84

T

talk therapy, 84–85
therapists, 72, 75, 78–79, 84–85
trauma cycle, 77–78
trigger events, 8, 77–79
Triggiano, Mary, 55

U

United States Congress, 72
unsubstantiated cases, 46
U.S. Department of Justice, 46

V

van der Kolk, Bessel, 72, 84
voluntary services, 52
Voorhees, Susan, 17

W

Webb, June, 62
Women, Infants, and Children (WIC) program, 19, 49

Y

yoga, 86–87

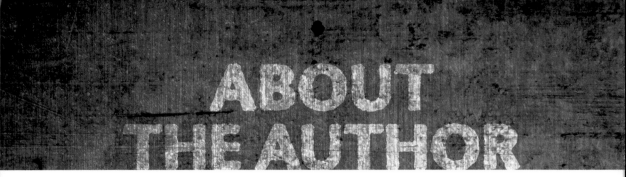

ABOUT THE AUTHOR

Allison Krumsiek is an author and poet living in Washington, D.C. She currently writes for a number of organizations, including nonprofits and the federal government, and she has also written other titles in Lucent's Hot Topics series. When she is not writing or editing, she can be found reading books or fearlessly defending her field hockey goal, but never at the same time.

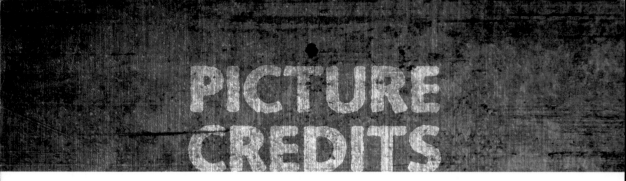

PICTURE CREDITS